# HAND IN HAND

ISBN: 978-0-9961558-6-1

Cover and interior design by Michele Barnes
Text set in Bodoni

MATTER PRESS
PO Box 704
Wynnewood, PA 19096
www.matterpress.com

# HAND IN HAND

MEG BOSCOV & RANDALL BROWN

FOR JONAH AND CHLOE, OUR BEST AND BRIGHTEST COLLABORATION

# TABLE OF CONTENTS

## TABLE OF CONTENTS CONTINUED

# INTRODUCTION: SUNDAY FOCUS

**W**elcome. Isn't that what the door offers?

This book developed out of a collaboration between a wife-and-husband team, the macro photographer Meg Boscov and the microfiction writer Randall Brown. Each Sunday, in the online literary magazine *The Journal of Compressed Creative Arts*, the feature "Sunday Focus" matches a photograph with a short inspirational message derived from the image. "Sunday Focus" has quickly become a popular feature. This book hopes to expand upon that initial vision.

Meg describes her work as the attempt to "capture beauty in nature both intrinsic and hidden"; Randall explains his as the attempt to "make something significant of something tiny."

Macro meets micro. Neither Meg nor Randall worries much about labels, such as this one from National Geographic: "Macro photography is photography magnified. It is generally recognized as 'macro' when you are increasing the size of an object in your picture from about half life-size, as represented on the image sensor, to five times life-size." Who has the time to measure?

The same is true of micro or flash fiction. When does something micro become something other: flash, drabble, dribble, quick, sudden, short, short short, and on and on. So many labels to rip off of things, aren't there?

Oh, that door. *Knock. Knock.*

Does it beckon? Doors create thresholds, and thresholds create threshold guardians—as Joseph Campbell called them—"guardians who protect the Special World and its secrets and provide essential tests to prove the would-be threshold-crosser's commitment and worth."

Think of all the doors Dorothy encounters: the door to the storm shelter closed against her, the door opening to Oz, the door to the Emerald City, the door protecting the wizard.

Remember Grover's fear of discovering the monster at the end of the book, only to find out that the monster is Grover himself? The door opens, revealing a mirror. Who's there? It's you.

In childhood, on Electric Company, a plumber endlessly knocked on a door to the great joy of a parrot inside. "Who is it?" the parrot cawed. "It's the plumber. I've come to fix the sink." To which, a hundred, thousand, million times, the parrot responded, "Who is it?" To which, a million times minus one, the plumber responded, "It's the plumber. I've come to fix the sink."

Finding the collapsed plumber, the parrot's person asks outside the door, "Who is it?" "It was the plumber," the parrot says. "He's come to fix the sink."

*Who is it?*

It's the reader. I've come to…

Why did you open this door? What brought you here? What is that you've come to fix? There's much broken, isn't there?

In photographs and tiny fictions, we often find ourselves. It is our sincere hope that, within this book, you'll indeed find something of a mirror, some part of yourself to reflect upon.

This book…

…matches the picture worth a thousand words with around a thousand words, or however many fit on the single page across from it.

…contains 52 such matches, one for each week of the year; we suggest a Sunday.

…attempts to give you a bit of the surreal to go with your morning cereal.

…hopes to inspire you to create your own collections of words and images as a way to explore both your outer and inner environments.

…(hopefully) gives you multiple perspectives, a multitude of ways of seeing.

…ends with a carefully considered call to action for you to consider carefully.

It is crazy, perhaps, to write anything about these photographs, says Randall the writer, because they speak so strongly for themselves.

Jacques Lacan, the French psychoanalyst, has written that, because the words we use to capture the reality of our world have been placed upon the world arbitrarily, our words can never fully capture the truth of our existence.

But we try—word after word, sentence after sentence, breath after breath—to grasp an essence that will always elude us.

What else can we do, given the state of the world? We try.

# 1: ROTATE & REFLECT

**Rotate 90 degrees clockwise.** New perspectives await.

Here, we find reflection, from the Latin *flectere* (to bend) and *re* (back). The image captures that sense of bending back, as if to get a better look. The flower regards itself. For the sake of wisdom or out of vanity? That is the question.

The oracle of Apollo at Delphi demanded of the ancient Greek 'know thyself,' and mirrors have often been used as symbols of wisdom and self-knowledge. But Apollo also required 'nothing in excess,' and the mirror can just as easily imply vanity, an unhealthy amount of self-regard. The peril of over admiring one's mirror image is encapsulated in the ancient Greek myth of Narcissus, the beautiful boy who having fallen in love with his reflection in a pool, pined away and was turned into a flower.[1]

Out of the frame and off-stage of the Narcissus story is Echo, the woman who loved him. But, as we all know, he only had eyes for himself. She too transforms into a reflection, of sound instead of sight.

Isn't it interesting, you might be thinking, that the image itself was reflected within the camera. Even more interesting, perhaps, is that this image was shot using a "mirrorless camera."

In a mirrorless camera...

...light passes through the lens directly onto the image sensor, and the optical viewfinder is replaced with an electronic viewfinder that replicates the image sensor...Since everything is duplicated directly from the image sensor, camera settings such as white balance, saturation and contrast can be seen through the viewfinder directly and additional information overlays including live histograms can be placed within the viewfinder, allowing photographers to see exactly what they are about to take a picture of.[2]

To see exactly!
Isn't that why we bend back?
Yet, it is the artist's own vision, that inner world, that we see reflected in this image. Had I taken the shot, it would look entirely different, surely not as beautiful or otherworldly. It would look very much like a flower and water. Something very ordinary.

Of writing, Stephen King famously offered this:

Look—here's a table covered with red cloth. On it is a cage the size of a small fish aquarium. In the cage is a white rabbit with a pink nose and pink-rimmed eyes. [...] On its back, clearly marked in blue ink, is the numeral 8. [...] The most interesting thing here isn't even the carrot-munching rabbit in the cage, but the number on its back. Not a six, not a four, not nineteen-point-five. It's an eight. This is what we're looking at, and we all see it. I didn't tell you. You didn't ask me. I never opened my mouth and you never opened yours. We're not even in the same year together, let alone the same room...except we are together. We are close. We're having a meeting of the minds. [...] We've engaged in an act of telepathy. No mythy-mountain shit; real telepathy.[3]

Imagine if Narcissus' pool had been fouled. Would he still have seen his unearthly beauty?

For this first week, engage in telepathy. Begin with reflection, allowing the outer world to enter, and next color it with your own take. Then send it out to someone—a photo, a note, a memo, a text, a poem, a song, a story—and have a meeting of the minds.

The world might indeed be too fouled and fallen for Narcissus to fall for himself ever again. But allow your own reflections to wipe the world clean. Allow the rest of us to see exactly what world you are picturing, and maybe, just maybe we'll echo it back to you.

We might even call it love.

# 2: STEP IN A SUNSHINE DAYDREAM

*T*rippy.

Very trippy.

Like the shows from (my) childhood. Mr. Rogers' Neighborhood of Make-Believe. Willie Wonka. H.R. Pufnstuf. The Banana Splits. The New Zoo Revue.

Coming right at you.

Are those mushrooms dancing in the blur?

The image transports us, beams us up, takes us (I hope) to a happy place. In Eric Berne's psychedelic children's book *Happy Valley,* we get, at the end of the story, this exchange:

> "How do you change your mind?' asked the Princess.
>
> Shardlu didn't know how to answer that, but at that point Abe asked:
>
> "Does anybody want to know how to change your mind?
>
> All the animals shook their heads and said "No," as usual, so Abe said, "Well you go to the land of Rodamal, where everything is backward and inside out, and when you get back here your mind will be either backward or inside out, but not both."
>
> "How do you get there?" asked Flossie.

"You either swallow yourself or get to the other side of a mirror," answered Abe. "I was there myself when I was little."[4]

*I was there myself when I was little.* Before the trip begins, we must become little again, yes, like Alice, to fit into the entryway. We must transform our bodies, and perhaps the mind will follow. Either backward or inside out.

But surely not both.

Greek *psykhe* "mind." Add to this *deloun* "make visible, reveal," whose own root *dyeu* means "to shine."

*Psyche-delic.* Is its shine revealing new things to the mind or revealing new things already inside the mind? Is it projecting inward or outward?

"If God dropped acid," Stephen Wright asks, "would he see people?"

It was Toto that made Dorthy laugh, and saved her from growing gray as her other surroundings. Toto was not gray; he was a little black dog, with long, silky hair and small black eyes that twinkled merrily on either side of his funny, wee nose. Toto played all day long, and Dorothy played with him, and loved him dearly.[5]

Gray might be the color of our futures, not only as individuals ("The sun and wind had changed [Em] too. They had taken the sparkle from her eyes and left them a somber grey.") but as a civilization. We might take our trips not just to escape the gray, but to return the color back to our world, a world that has wasted its possibilities.

From Chicago in 1900, *Wizard of Oz* author L. Frank Baum wrote that the story "aspires to being a modernized fairy tale, in which the wonderment and joy are retained and the heart-aches and nightmares are left out."

My landlady in Chicago Leisa Mohr once told me, "When Karl and I were married, I sent a postcard home. You know what it said, my boy? This year I went around the world. Next year, I want to go someplace different."

The world, at times, needs a new place, one previously unexplored. Whether it's to a world right outside our windows or to the other side of the rainbow, a trip beckons us to escape the world that has become ho-hum, gray with worry.

This week, go someplace different.

UNTITLED   16

# 3: BESTOWING TITLES UPON SUBJECTS

What would you title this image? There is the "story" the photographer has shot and the one that the viewer sees. Does a title bridge the gap? Is that light in the distance the coming Apocalypse or a savior? From where did they set off? Who held whose hand first?

The title imposes a kind of order, a kind of focus. The title usually lives outside the frame, the characters unaware of the claim it imposes upon them.

Does Nick know that Fitzgerald named his book *The Great Gatsby?* Likely not, or there might've been a lawsuit. The title exists for you—the reader, the viewer, a gift from the creator.

And why, always, is there that desire to create a narrative, a story, as a way to make meaning of the world?

Narrative capability shows up in infants some time in their third or fourth year, when they start putting verbs together with nouns. Its appearance coincides, roughly, with the first memories that are retained by adults of their infancy, a conjunction that has led some to propose that memory itself is dependent on the capacity for narrative. In other words, we do not have any mental record of who we are until narrative is present as a kind of armature, giving shape to that record… The gift of narrative is so pervasive and universal that there are those who strongly suggest that narrative is a 'deep structure,' a

human capacity genetically hard-wired into our minds in the same way as our capacity for grammar (according to some linguists) is something we are born with.[6]

We are born with the template for narrative; and the rest of our lives is spent filling that template, putting verbs to nouns, actions to things, much as we might fill a backpack in preparation for a journey, stuffing it with all the desires we might, if given the right moment, enact.

Story is a meaning-making mechanism. In this image of father and daughter, notice how right away I'm imposing a meaning/story onto the figures, giving them their positions, their titles: Father & Daughter. They hold each other and our attentions. Why? The archetype of father and daughter pulls at those buried structures, pulling up long-forgotten feelings from the depths.

How quickly one of the hands becomes mine—or does it become both? Parent and child.

Is it the parent-self holding the hand of the child-self? The image leads to a story leads to me seeing myself in it, the emotions of "parent" and "child" tugging me along.

Parent. Child. The archetypes alone exert their power over emotions.

What is their story? You tell me.

I love that little backpack, don't you? Maybe that's where story lives. Maybe that's your way in.

The filmmaker Charlie Kaufman writes, "I like titles that are a little difficult, because it's kind of counterintuitive." We think of titles as imposing some final order, telling us exactly what something is, as we did with our high school papers, titling them "The Tragedy in *King Lear*" or "The Causes of the Vietnam War."

And that is a fine way to title things. But titles might surprise you. As you look at this image, what titles come to mind? Does the title "Last Touch" create a different story? What about "Letting Go"?

This week, bestow titles to your visions. What would you title that dream?—that scene at the grocery store?—that flutter of hummingbird at the feeder?—that sound outside your window?

Bestow titles upon your visitors, your neighbors, your landscapes, the figures in your gardens.

Give shape. Make meaning. Go deep. Surprise yourself.

# 4: START AN ALGORITHM REVOLUTION

*D*id you know that digital cameras, such as the ones used to shoot these images, modify each picture before presenting it to the user?

Here Marilyn Wolf explains the decisions the "smart" camera makes about processing an image:

Better pictures require good algorithms. But those algorithms make decisions about how to process the picture to get the 'best' results. And 'best' is clearly a subjective criterion. I believe that at the heart of the digital camera revolution is the move from previsualization by the photographer to autoprevisualization by the camera. Previsualization is a term introduced by Ansel Adams—he taught photographers to see in the their mind's eye how they wanted their photo to look and then determine the proper combination of techniques to achieve that result. Previsualization is a human, artistic endeavor. Cameras cannot make that sort of profound artistic judgments that Ansel Adams did, but they can make choices based on scene characteristics and knowledge about the composition of typical photographs.[7]

For the images in this book, the photographer used Lightroom and Photoshop not so much to manipulate, but rather to return that previsualization to a human, artistic endeavor—to undo (some of) the decisions made by the algorithms—and return the image to the one seen by the photographer in her mind's eye.

And also to clean up dirt and blemishes. Who knew how messy a petal could get?

A postmodern thinker (or are we are at post-post modernism?) might be thinking how we too have algorithms in our brains that manipulate our thinking of the world, our selves, continually modifying each bit of information we take in. How did the algorithms arise? Are they embedded in language?—culture?—media?—all things? And how, if we want, can we undo the decisions those algorithms have been making for us?

Art!

Of course.

Art!

In photograph after photograph, as I page through this book, I am in wonder. Someone sees the world like this! Or rather, to someone, the world appears as such.

It's possible for the world to look like this! It is. Oh my, it really is.

The world transforms, as if the "matrix" has been revealed, removed, the algorithms overridden. Digital cameras and their calculations don't want you to see the world like this, but you beat them, went around them.

A revolution.

What algorithms have been planted within your mechanisms? Imagine what the world might look like, feel like, sound like, taste like, smell like without those re-calculations taking place without your input.

Imagine how sad the world would be without this artistic curating that recovers perception from someone else's idea of what is "best." Imagine seeing the garden as I once saw it. Like this:

Try this. Write for 15 minutes without stopping about these questions above, without concern about grammar or sense. Without concern about answers.

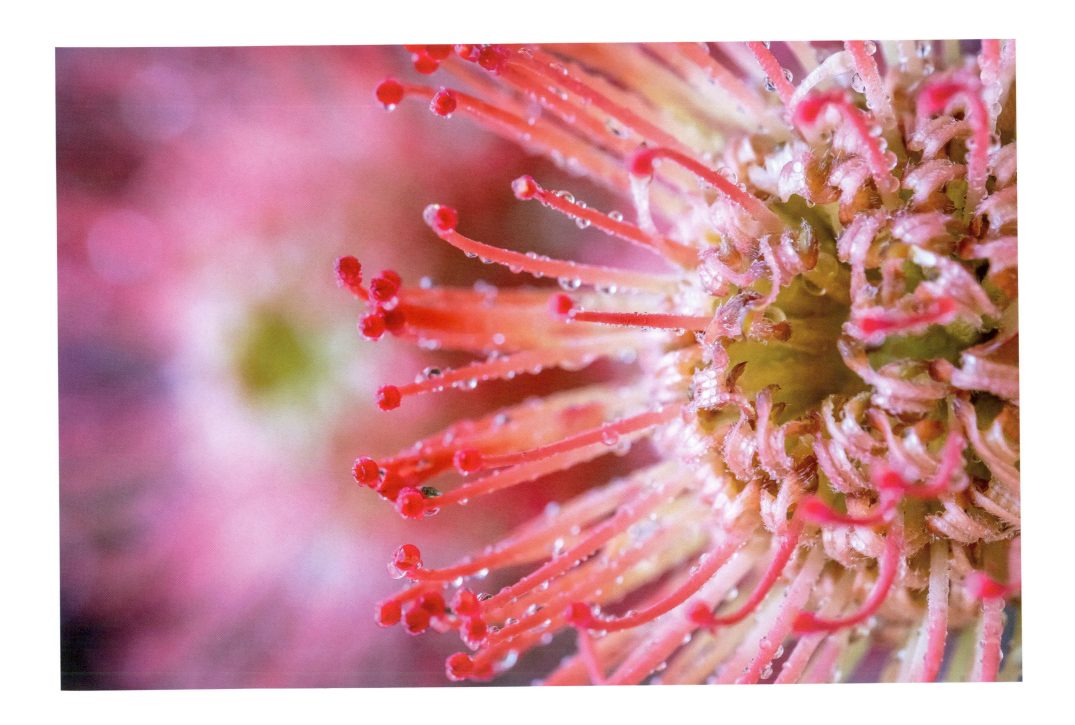

# 5: SEE CREATURE, BE CREATURE

 requently, the images from the protean world of the backyard garden take on an under-the-sea quality. They look like some unbefore identified creature from the depths.

A popular writing assignment invites students to draw a monster, and then either (1) to describe the monster in writing or (2) to describe why that image is thought of as a monster.

Who or what makes the monster a monster?

Who looks at an image or a someone and sees "creature"?

And what is that creature doing in the garden?

In my head, the Disney song "Under the Sea" has been playing on an endless loop since I wrote "under-the-sea." Ariel is a strange sea creature, a young mermaid, a princess who lives in this world below the surface full of wonder after wonder.

"What more is you lookin' for," Sebastian sings to Ariel, as a way to keep her drowned under the habits and conventions of the world.

*Creature* has at its root, the O.E.D. tells us, post-classical Latin *creatura*: anything created, the created universe, creation.[8]

This image is a creature, these words are creatures, this book is a creature full of other creatures. Creatures of love. Do you hear David Byrne's voice yet?

 Every image embodies a way

of seeing. Even a photograph. For photographs are not, as is often assumed, a mechanical record. Every time we look at a photograph, we are aware, however slightly, of the photographer selecting that sight from an infinity of other possible sights. This is true even in the most casual family snapshot. The photographer's way of seeing is reflected in [her] choice of subject.[9]

 Our photographer sees the fantastical, producing impossible creature after impossible creature, an under-the-sea organism thriving in the baked sun of a summer garden. How can this be? It is her way of seeing that the image has captured, a way of being, an openness to wonder.

In *Way of the Sacred*, Francis Huxley writes the following:

If [we are] to thrust [our heads] through the appearances of this world— through the customary scenery of [our] own habits and the conventions of [our] society—[we] must for a time abandon any simple ideas of machinery. What is beyond conceptualizing may then present itself to [our] naked minds, perhaps as a void full of unmannerly energies, a darkness without bottom, or a light that cannot be withstood; perhaps as an enormous and disreputable joke perpetrated upon [humankind]; or perhaps as an exquisite harmony of contradictions—

like the burning bush seen by Moses, that burned with fire and yet was not consumed.[10]

We yearn to see "what is beyond conceptualizing," that vision taking the form of concordant contradictions, like a fantastical creature that is neither fantastical nor a creature.

 ...Photography is a form of magic. It has the ability to do so much more than simply show us what something or someone looks like. Photography—great photography—manages to penetrate the surface of the world and show us a little of what lies beneath.[11]

This week, see with your naked mind, see a creature—something created by your seeing it.

Ariel answers Sebastian's *what more you lookin for?* with her own voice, the sonorous "I want to be...I want to see." This week, you might answer Sebastian's question with an attempt to see what is beyond, to see the fantastical in the customary scenery of the everyday.

 This week, see creature.
Break on through.
Break on through.
And show us what you see on the other side.

# 6: ENCOUNTER WILD DESIRES

*I*t's alive! It's alive!
It's reaching towards us.
What does it want?
What everyone wants.
Love?

Or maybe it's just hungry.

Many of our most profound, life-affecting desires are not rational, in the sense that we don't use rational thought processes to form them. Indeed, we don't form them; they form themselves within us…A single rogue desire can trample the plans we had for our lives and thereby alter our destinies.[12]

In story-world, an inciting incident pushes a repressed desire to the surface, forcing a character into a series of actions to fulfill that single rogue desire, trampling all that comes before it. Desire tingles at the ends of those purple feelers. What has happened to incite such yearning? What is the new thing that has arrived?

In *Who Am I?*, Steven Reiss lists 16 basic desires: power, independence, curiosity, acceptance, order, saving, honor, idealism, social contact, family, status, vengeance, romance, eating, physical activity, and tranquility.[13]

We never know when the lens will find us.
Never know which desire will be incited.

Nonrational and only marginally in our control, desire lurks in the margins, like the monsters in our childhood closets, waiting for us let our guard down.
Out of the blue, they spring upon us.
What is that they want, beyond fulfillment? Connection, perhaps? Maybe they push their purple feelers outward—hungry, empty, eager, keen.
How do we connect to our desires? How are they revealed to us?
Perhaps in conflicts, in challenging ourselves.
Perhaps in stillness, in discovering ourselves.
Perhaps in the images our mind projects on the screen of our sleep. In dreams.

In describing the works of Jacques Lacan, Leader and Groves discuss how our dreams reveal our desires: "Desire itself will emerge in little details…What really matters is why, in your dream, the supposed fulfillment has taken the form of a four-poster bed and a bowl of a caviar."[14]
"A great work of art is like a dream," writes Jung. "For all its apparent obviousness it does not explain itself and is never unequivocal. A dream never says: 'You ought', or: 'This is the truth.' It presents an image in much the same way as nature allows a plant to grow, and we must draw our own conclusions."[15]

Why is this image the one that gets the heading "Wild Desires"? What can we learn by looking at the little details? We must, as the great Jung says, all draw our own conclusions.
For this week, focus on desire. Look at the little details of your dreams. Why have they taken on this form? What quirk, what transformation, what twist has the deep embedded desire undergone in its journey from the deep recesses of your unconscious to the light? Why, for example, has my wish to publish my novel taken on the form, in dreams, of trying to catch a fly ball, the old, worn catcher's mitt of my grandfather in full-focus?
To what art are you drawn? What desires reveal themselves in the tiny details? What do those purple feelers want? What might they grasp should they ever reach you?
And what would you do?
Run?
Or embrace.

# 7: TAKE A LOOK INSIDE

*Outside of a dog, a book is a man's best friend. Inside of a dog it's too dark to read.* —Groucho Marx

Outside, presents are wrapped tight, held in confidence, hidden away. Inside, the gifts wait in silence, wait for the ripping of the wrapping paper, for the great reveal.

Inside, like the flicker of flame.
Inside, like the inhale of breath.
Inside, like the flutter of heartbeats.

In describing Maurice Merleau-Ponty's philosophy of the inside, Sarah Bakewell writes,

When he looks for his own metaphor to describe how he sees consciousness, he comes up with a beautiful one: consciousness, he suggests, is like a 'fold' in the world, as though someone had crumpled a piece of cloth to make a little nest or hollow. It stays for a while, before eventually being unfolded and smoothed away.[16]

Inside a hollow.
Inside a nest.
Inside a fold in the world.

and I, in my brand new body, / which was not a woman's yet, / told the stars my questions / and thought God could really see / the heat and the painted light, / elbows, knees, dreams, goodnight.[17]

Inside, there's consciousness. A flickering stillness. A gift.

Inside a closet I found the Kiddie City receipt for all my holiday gifts. My parents, not Santa, had been responsible, not only for that year's presents, but all nine of the previous years'. I didn't know, until then, that they had such a thing within them. I had no idea they could keep secrets, play pretend, create mythologies.

Until then, I thought they were pretty ho-hum.

But your vision will become clear only when you can look into your own heart. Without, everything seems discordant; only within does it coalesce into unity. Who looks outside dreams; who looks inside awakes.[18]

Inside, awake and folded in, like a baby bird in the nest, mouth open, anticipating.

Immediately, Mrs. Ramsay seemed to fold herself together, one petal closed in another, and the whole fabric fell in exhaustion upon itself, so that she had only strength enough to move her finger, in exquisite abandonment to exhaustion, across the page of Grimm's fairy story, while there throbbed through her, like the pulse in a spring which has expanded to its full width and now gently ceases to beat, the rapture of successful creation.[19]

Helen Keller writes, "Once I knew only darkness and stillness...my life was without past or future... but a little word from the fingers of another fell into my hand that clutched at emptiness, and my heart leaped to the rapture of living."[20]

This week, look inside: a box, a closet, a flower, a door, a dark corner, your self.

As you do so, look at what you've awakened. Feed it.

# 8: WONDER AT THE FIRST PASSION

*I* wonder: Is your spider-sense tingling?

✕

"I regard wonder," writes Descartes in *Passions of the Soul*, "as the first of all passions. It has no opposite; for, if the object before us has no characteristics that surprise us, we are not moved by it at all and we consider it without passion."[21]

✕

As the magazine *Discover* explains, the web begins its wondrous existence by waiting for the wind:

To begin a web, a spider anchors a strand of dragline silk—three times stronger than the Kevlar in bulletproof vests—and waits for a breeze to blow it to a second attachment point. The arachnid then completes the outer ring and spokes, and finally builds the spiral.[22]

✕

I wonder: Is it also that same wind that will come to destroy the web?

✕

After paralyzing its prey, some spiders may wrap it up in silk to make it easier to transport back to the nest. Some species actually cover the prey in silk before injecting the venom, making it easier to attack. A female spider may carry wrapped prey back to its young spiderlings, and a male may bring the wrapped prey to a female as a courtship gift.[23]

✕

I picture the female spider opening this gift wrapped in silk. Does she peel away strand after strand gently or hungrily?

Is she moved by it? Does she always fall madly in love?

✕

"The artist is a receptacle for emotions that come from all over the place: from the sky, from the earth, from a scrap of paper, from a passing shape, from a spider's web." —Pablo Picasso[24]

✕

Walt Whitman writes of a "noiseless patient spider" on a tiny point of land in the midst of the ocean, launching forth "filament, filament, filament." In the poem, Whitman wonders if this spider is like his soul, "ceaselessly musing, venturing, throwing, seeking" until the "gossamer thread…catch somewhere."[25]

Wonder originates in the soul, remains bound to it, our senses shivering along the gossamer threads that connect soul-to-sense, vibrating, tingling, catching.

✕

Go in search of wonder, in search of an object that surprises the senses, moves the passions. I am sure that day our photographer left her home, she wasn't going in search of spiders. She wasn't looking for them; instead, she began seeing them.

"If you want to take great pictures," writes Henry Carroll, "ones that really stand out, you need to stop looking and start *seeing*." To see, Carroll argues, one must focus on "personal approaches, feeling, and rethinking."[26]

In other words, one must wander into wonder, relying on one's instincts, one's heart, one's own understanding of the rules.

✕

Somewhere, a gust of wind has caught a strand of silk; somewhere that silk launches, filament, filament, filament, hoping to catch.

That thread pulls on your soul.

A gift.

This week, catch that first breeze, follow it deeply and quickly, before that final breeze blows, taking everything with it.

# 9: DELIVER UP SOME SOFT SERVE

 Whenever I had collected enough change from the sofa cushions, I'd pedal my purple Schwinn with Pirates' cards clothes-pinned in the spokes to the Dairy Queen on the Carlisle Pike for a Mister Misty Freeze: grape slush with vanilla soft serve ice cream. Nectar of the gods and goddesses.

*Soft as misted star.*
   —Mary Louisa Anderson

*Soft as a sunny shadow*
*When day is almost done.*
   —Christina Georgina Rossetti

*Soft as Muses' string.*
   —Elizabeth Barrett Browning

*Soft as pity.*
   —George Darley

*Soft as sleep.*
   —Hesiod

*Soft as love's first word.*
   —Jean Ingelow

*Softer than the West wind's sigh.*
   —Percy Bysshe Shelley[27]

On early Sunday mornings, my brother and I would play tennis at the local public courts with my father and a family friend, who was highly competitive. The kids versus the grown-ups. Whenever my brother or I would rush the net, the family friend would drill forehands at our precious parts; she aimed for far corners and the edges of lines. At set point, she screaming at him to administer the knockout punch, my father would deliver to us the softest serve.

The funny thing about the heart is a soft heart is a strong heart, and a hard heart is a weak heart.
   —Criss Jami, *Healology*[28]

Softly, I'd tread around my grandfather, asleep with the Saturday Western on the television, John Wayne lifting his niece as if to dash her upon the rocks, only to hold her in his soft embrace. My grandfather's soft snores, his soft hands like the webbing of the leather Spalding catcher's mitt he'd given me for Christmas, his soft whisper as he awoke. *What I miss?*

*Softly as moonlight steals upon the skies.*
   —Julia C. R. Dorr

*Softly … as music that floats through a dream.*
   —Minnie Gilmore

*Softly as full-blown flower*
*Unfolds its heart to welcome in the dawn.*
   —Henry Van Dyke[29]

*When you are old and gray and full of sleep, and nodding by the fire, take down this book and slowly read, and dream of the soft look your eyes had once, and of their shadows deep.*
   —William Butler Yeats[30]

This week, serve up something soft.
As soft as stars.
As soft as shadows.
As soft as strings.
As sleep.
As the West wind's sigh.
As an unfolding heart.
As the look your eyes had once, the new-found change chiming with each piston-like pedal across the A&P parking lot, toward the promise of the Mr. Misty Freeze, the hard-earned reward of that hard, hard childhood.

# 10: ADDRESS THE BLUR

es, it's time to address the elephant in the room. Bokeh.

**bo·keh**
noun

the visual quality of the out-of-focus areas of a photographic image, especially as rendered by a particular lens.

The blur! The blur! Yes, it has a name. Of course it has a name. "Bokeh," the fine folks at Nikon tell us, "comes from the Japanese word *boke* (ボケ), which means 'blur' or 'haze', or *boke-aji*, the 'blur quality.'"[31]

Harsh transforms to soft; bright to diffused. "Always two there are," Yoda tells us, "no more, no less." Two sides: focus & blur. Apollonian and Dionysian.

Art is born out of as well as encapsulates the continuing battle between order and chaos. It seeks order or form, even when portraying anarchy. It's a tension visible in both Greek statuary and the colour field paintings of Rothko and Newman, stopping off at every conceivable artistic movement in between. It's a tension that arises from our natural urge to reconcile opposites. When Friedrich Nietzsche declared in *The Birth of Tragedy* that 'art owes its continuous evolution to the Apollonian–Dionysian duality', he was implicitly declaring his belief that the tensions between form and content, head and heart, discipline and desire were the building blocks of dramatic structure.[32]

"What makes photography a strange invention," John Berger writes, "is that its primary raw materials are light and time."[33]

Light and dark. Movement and stillness. The tick tock of time and the silence of nothingness.

Always two there are.

We are all engaged in a balancing act, no more, no less.

Milan Kundera writes in *The Book of Laugher and Forgetting*, "…Whereas the devil's laughter denoted the absurdity of things, the angel on the contrary meant to rejoice over how well ordered, wisely conceived, good, and meaningful everything here below was."[34]

Within the world exists two powerful competing desires, a Dionysian need to raze the world and uncover its meaninglessness—and the opposing Apollonian wish to reconstruct the world and rediscover its deep meaning and purpose.

One force focuses.
The other blurs.

The Apollonian imposes definitions, boundaries, rules, borders, labels, civilization, society, culture, orchards, knowledge, adulthood, cities and towns, hearths and kilns, dictionaries and libraries; it imposes rationality upon the world and all its terrible wonders.

Bokeh is…one of those 'perfectly imperfect' touches that can make a photo seem at the same time effortless and intentional…Let all that light play around in the out-of-focus portions of your shot. Play is the key word here.[35]

Chaos. That world before creation, the void—"And the earth was without form, and void; and darkness was upon the face of the deep"—the world before the Spirit "moved upon the face of the waters."

It is matter without meaning or intent.
It is.

This week, turn up the blur to "11." Play it loud and often.

And may the bokeh be with you.

# 11: WELCOME A TRICKSTER

*W*hat do you see in the shadows?

A form?
Is it dancing?
Changing shapes?
Is it human?
Or is it something else?
A trickster, perhaps?

Kokopelli is one of the most easily recognized figures found in the petroglyphs and pictographs of the Southwest. The earliest known petroglyph of the figure dates to about 1000 AD....[and] the Hopi Kokopelli was often represented by a human dancer.[36]

Tricksters take many forms; Bugs Bunny, for example. "While one prominent feature of the trickster's personality is gender ambiguity," writes Mills, "the trickster is almost always conceived in Western comparative theory as a male who can transform or disguise himself as a female, usually with comical and highly disorderly results. But the 'female' trickster, in typical trickster fashion, was always there, invisible to the patriarchy."[37]

Finding a trickster on every page, behind every tree, at every river bank, might seem to be a literary obsession. Then again, it might begin a journey towards redefining Native American literature, oral and written; American literature, native and non-native, canonical and marginal, male and female. In fact, looking for [a] trickster in unlikely places might just produce the kind of chaotic disordering so characteristic of [a] trickster who eludes, disrupts, and defies classifications of any kind. Messing around, on and with boundaries, is risky, daring and delicate business.[38]

Fluid in their movements, the trickster dances, and you might think the trickster stirs up chaos only to blur conventional boundaries. But tricksters use their tricks also to save us, becoming "culture-heroes," stealing fire from the heavens to give to humankind, for example.

This photo, perhaps, gives us a rare image of the trickster, captured mid-dance. I imagine tricksters perpetually in motion, a blur of wile.

To Yoda, who says always two there are, the trickster might bring some boundary-blurring fluidity into this vision that sees the world as binary-bound.

The trickster enters this book to disorder everything that came before.

The trickster comes to save the culture from its own blindness.

The trickster shines a light on the chains that keep us all from being as free, as risky, as daring, as delicate.

For this week, let in the trickster. Let tricksters do their chaotic disordering. Allow them to clutter. Look for them in the most unlikely of places, upending all you thought you knew.

Like Bugs, she might be hiding in Room 2B.
2B or not 2B?
Of course, such a binary question shouldn't be the end-all & be-all. This week, be all you can be by upending a binary or two. Or three.

# 12: DANCE IF U WANT 2

The image twirls.
Dances!
Yes, it's here.
Twirl-time.
Dance this mess around.

We can see the magic in this shot of the "twirl." "Ordinary nature" transforms into the supernatural, the physical form twirls up and up into the realm of the spirit. Feel the delight in "being." Feel the forces of the friendly twirling, twirling, casting its spell, summoning.

Dance, dance, dance.

*To watch us dance is to hear our hearts speak.*
—Hopi aphorism

*Everything in the universe has rhythm. Everything dances.* —Maya Angelou

*Don't look at your feet to see if you are doing it right. Just dance.*—Anne Lamott

Dancing is not an invention of [humankind], since birds and monkeys dance…No animal or primitive human being dances unless urged by some specific excitement, and before the excitement dies down and the dancer relaxes [her] efforts, the dance transforms the excitement into ecstasy. Ecstasy enhances the physical strength of the dancer and changes [her] mentality… In losing consciousness of [her] ordinary nature [she] feels within [herself] a superhuman power which raises [her] to the stature of a spirit; and as a spirit [she] believes [she] is able to control the forces of nature, to summon friendly and to banish hostile powers. Thus, the dances… are magic actions and in consequence constructed in such a manner as to achieve a magic purpose.[39]

Magic actions to achieve a magic purpose. Losing a self-consciousness and self-awareness to dance with the spirits. To lose one's self in order to find it. Again and again.

Twirl…like atoms in the sunshine. What is magic, anyways? A power? Yes. A power "to influence the course of events or to manipulate the natural world."

Is that why, as kids, magic and those who wielded it attracted so much of our attentions?

Power. Transformation. Transcendence.
To leave our bodies and the world.
To twirl above it all.
Free.

*Faeries, come take me out of this dull world,*
*For I would ride with you upon the wind,*
*Run on the top of the dishevelled tide,*
*And dance upon the mountains like a flame.*
—William Butler Yeats[40]

What spell does this twirling image hope to summon? What power does it seek? What spheres? What dance does it dance?
They do the Purple Kirtle.
Do the Laverne Twirl.
Do the Transcendental.
Do the Unconcerned Whorl.

"Hey now," as the B52s shout, "don't that make you feel a whole lot better?"

Create your own dance. Give it a name. Give it a whirl. Summon some spirits. Call upon the flower powers to take you with them on some far-off fancy.

Do the Succulent Shake.
Do the Botanical Quake.
Do the Intangible.
Do the Cauliflower.
Do the Terrible Beauty.
Do the Southward Shuffle.
Do it all.

# 13: REPAIR THE BROKEN

Seeing the crack of the butterfly's wing, Meg wanted both to highlight and repair it; she waited for the moment that the flowers joined the wing's break, engaging herself in the traditional art of *Kintsugi*:

> When a bowl, teapot or precious vase falls and breaks into a thousand pieces, we throw them away angrily and regretfully. Yet there is an alternative, a Japanese practice that highlights and enhances the breaks thus adding value to the broken object. It's called *kintsugi* (金継) or *kintsukuroi* (金繕い), literally golden ('kin') and repair ('tsugi').
>
> This traditional Japanese art uses a precious metal—liquid gold, liquid silver or lacquer dusted with powdered gold—to bring together the pieces of a broken pottery item and at the same time enhance the breaks. The technique consists in joining fragments and giving them a new, more refined aspect. Every repaired piece is unique, because of the randomness with which ceramics shatters and the irregular patterns formed that are enhanced with the use of metals.[41]

During our wedding, as per the Jewish custom, Meg and I at the end of the ceremony were to smash a glass. (I missed the glass and smashed her toes, a literal way of getting a marriage off on the wrong foot). In researching the meaning of the glass-smash, I came across the idea that the glass represents the current shattered state of the world, kind of like the world post-Eden.

What should we do with the broken, scattered fragments?

I imagine that many of us would like to put the glass together invisibly, so that it appears complete, fully formed, rather pristine. But what if we take up the shards of the shattered world and piece them together in some new form, with the cracks and the process of sequencing them visible (broken-ness that is aware of itself as broken)?

Here, the broken is brought together with the beautiful: those purple petals that do not replace the hole in the wing but instead retain it.

The butterfly and its broken-ness become part of the powdered petals; the petals, part of the butterfly.

Something precious fills in the gaps.

As a writer of very small fictions, seeing those fragments, I might choose what could be considered a third way: brevity. The writer of tiny fictions picks up one of these shards and views it as complete in itself. Working within the incompleteness of that space, the writer creates something whole. Maybe that, too, is a way of filling the broken with something precious.

Any way you choose simultaneously to heal and highlight the broken, the Japanese concept of *wabi-sabi* is something to consider.

"It's a very complex idea, but part of *wabi-sabi* is about holding imperfection above perfection," the artist Joseph Weaver explains. "Everyone can relate to flaws, which may be why people find this art form particularly compelling. They see themselves in the work."[42]

This week, repair the broken with something precious, something that highlights and values the individual pieces and the cracks that have grown between and among them.

Engage in *kintsugi*.

And in doing so, in embracing *wabi-sabi*, we might be embracing our own breaks, our own incompleteness, our own nature, filling it by repairing the world around us, by filling the breaks with gold.

The "hardest hue to hold."[43]

# 14: LIFT UP BUT NEVER AWAY

The tiny flower lifts up its petals to the bigger one above.

Do you see a child lifting its tiny hands to their parent?

Hear the whisper:

Up.

Up.

Up, mommy, up.

That reach for mommy. So lovely. So powerful in its archetypal pull:

As a newborn, your baby probably kept her fingers curled into tiny little fists. But it won't be long before she realizes she has hands and arms that are pretty darn good at grabbing for things. When your baby wants something, she'll learn to reach for it. And the first time your little one reaches for you from her crib? Your heart will melt.[44]

Up. Does the child want to fly? To be in the wind, held in the breath of the world? Up. Out of the crib and into the arms of mommy.

Of being all grown-up? Not so fast. Please.

Tiny everything.

Tiny fingers. Tiny toes. Tiny ears. Tiny nose.

To embrace something so tiny, so fragile, so new,

…as lambs

…as a flower

…as grace itself.[45]

Often, accompanied by those raised hands asking for "up" is a cry:

…And now you try

Your handful of notes;

The clear vowels rise like balloons.[46]

Up, too, those notes rise, caught by the wind. The world's breath catches the child's breath catches the mommy's ear, sends her up and running.

Even our little dog Hazel, with that first crack of thunder, cries, puts her paws into the air.

Up!

Swaddle me.

Care for me.

Help me.

Save me.

Love me.

Bring me up to your grown-up world.

Where it's safe.

Where it's warm.

Where I can lick your face.

The baby goes down to sleep. "So dawn goes down to day."[47] The tiny infant face sinks into slumber.

This book attempts to celebrate things that might otherwise be overlooked, be diminished.

Those tiny petals.

That tiny reach.

A seemingly tiny moment.

Looming so infinitely large.

This week, the image says, "Up."

Pick up something tiny.

Hold it close.

Feel its fragility, its need of your warmth.

Let it rest against you.

Let it lick your face.

# 15: LIGHTEN DARKNESS VISIBLE

In this passage, from William Styron's memoir of depression and madness *Darkness Visible*, he describes the night which he has decided will be his last, the night from which he will not wake, the night he has decided to end his life:

But even a few words came to seem to me too long-winded, and I tore up all my efforts, resolving to go out in silence. Late one bitterly cold night, when I knew that I could not possibly get myself through the following day, I sat in the living room of the house bundled up against the chill; something had happened to the furnace. My wife had gone to bed, and I had forced myself to watch the tape of a movie in which a young actress, who had been in a play of mine, was cast in a small part. At one point in the film, which was set in late-nineteenth-century Boston, the characters moved down the hallway of a music conservatory, beyond the walls of which, from unseen musicians, came a contralto voice, a sudden soaring passage from the Brahms *Alto Rhapsody*.

This sound, which like all music—indeed, like all pleasure—I had been numbly unresponsive to for months, pierced my heart like a dagger, and in a flood of swift recollection I thought of all the joys the house had known: the children who had rushed through its rooms, the festivals, the love and work, the honestly earned slumber, the voices and the nimble commotion, the perennial tribe of cats and dogs and birds, 'laughter and ability and Sighing, / And Frocks and Curls.' All this I realized was more than I could ever abandon, even as what I had set out so deliberately to do was more than I could inflict on those memories, and upon those, so close to me, with whom the memories were bound. And just as powerfully I realized I could not commit this desecration on myself. I drew upon some last gleam of sanity to perceive the terrifying dimensions of the mortal predicament I had fallen into. I woke up my wife and soon telephone calls were made. The next day I was admitted to the hospital.[48]

What will be that light that shines through to save us during our darkest times? And will it come from a faraway messenger, someone who left us with this saving message without any knowledge of sending it out to us, of the power it might have over us, the power to pierce our hearts, providing us one last powerful gleam of sanity?

Maybe you will receive such a message. Maybe you already have.

Late one bitterly cold night, Stryon pops a movie into his VCR, not knowing it will save his lie.

Oh, humanity!

All this, writes Styron, was more than he could ever abandon.

Humanity powerfully calls out to him.

Hold on! Hold on!

For him, the call toward the light began with a sound, sudden and soaring.

Sent in 1869.

*Then refresh his heart!*
*Open his clouded gaze*
*To the thousand springs*
*Next to the thirsting one*
*In the desert!*

This week, create your own message for some unknown recipient, a message for someone who might've entered a place with "no light, but rather darkness visible." It could be a letter, a recipe, a photograph, a poem, a story, a joke, a song, anything.

Put it in a bottle.

Send it out to the world.

We'll be waiting.

# 16: CONSIDER THE MOON

The moon brings with it a whole range of creatures, from aliens to the Zduhać, the aye-aye to the wombat. As Clark explains in 1914,

> Nocturnal animals, properly speaking, are animals which, while capable of performing all their normal functions in the day time, and not dependent upon other nocturnal animals, are active only at night.[49]

The nightwalkers! Predators, it seems, fill the night, both natural and unnatural, alive and undead, hunting, as if night symbolizes a lightless, spiritless world, the primordial darkness before Someone, or Something, turned on the lights.

But what fun night was! As kids, at night, we brought out the punk sticks, holding them in our mouths. We played "Wolf," a dressed-up hide-and-seek, capture the flag kind of game. We lit small fires and toasted campfire apple pies. In the night, the tiniest twig-crack could create terror; the smallest stray thought could invoke the feeling to run, run, as fast as your little legs could carry you to the nearest open door and the lights shining inside.

As a grown-up, a night out means some strange sounding cocktail, like "A Lonely Island Lost in the Middle of a Foggy Sea" or a "Monkey Gland."[50] It means coming home to a sleeping house (hopefully!), some final hour of quietude.

And over it all hangs the moon, the 5th largest in our solar system (my mnemonic device for remembering the order of plants being *My Very Enthusiastic Mother Just Served Us Noodles*). Bye, bye Pluto. The moon, on average, sits 238,857 miles away, orbiting the Earth every 27.3 days. According to the History Channel,

> Legends from various traditions around the world, including Buddhism and Native American folklore, recount the tale of a rabbit that lives on the moon. This shared myth may reflect common interpretations of markings on the lunar surface–an alternate take on the fabled 'man in the moon.'[51]

So that is what the owl in the backyard forest is hooting at all night long. The bunny on the moon! It all makes sense now.

What is it that the bunny on the moon sees as she rises to create the nocturnal world? Here's Emily Dickinson's take on that moment, from crescent to full face:

The Moon was but a Chin of Gold
A Night or two ago—
And now she turns Her perfect Face
Upon the World below—

Her Forehead is of Amplest Blonde—
Her Cheek—a Beryl hewn—
Her Eye unto the Summer Dew
The likest I have known—

Her Lips of Amber never part—
But what must be the smile
Upon Her Friend she could confer
Were such Her Silver Will—

And what a privilege to be
But the remotest Star—
For Certainty She take Her Way
Beside Your Palace Door—

Her Bonnet is the Firmament—
The Universe—Her Shoe—
The Stars—the Trinkets at Her Belt—
Her Dimities—of Blue—

This week, consider the moon. Consider what the bunny in her bonnet sees from her perch. Go out for a night.

Get nocturnal. Become a nightwalker. Then make a sprint for the light of home.

The Oxford English Dictionary indeed has an entry for *photobomb*:

To spoil (a photograph) by appearing unexpectedly in the camera's field of view as the picture is taken, typically as a prank or practical joke.[52]

Spoil the photograph! I think these two dudes in the background might disagree. "Spoiled it? Surely," they might say, "we've made it better."

The photobomber lives an ironic life, constantly acting to spoil things, only instead so often making the photo into something unexpectedly and interestingly embellished.

The act to photo-ruin creates something even more photo-worthy.

That rustle in the background!

It's a bird!

It's a flame!

No, it's an onomatopoeic [the way the *rustle* rustles] & ironic [the way the act to spoil does the exact opposite] photobomb.

Super, man.

The foreground flower seems to turn its head, as if looking, as if aware of the shenanigans going on behind it.

"Hey, hey, you two in the back, get your own shot. This one's mine!"

"We're da bomb," they yell back. "As in, *the really cool dudes wrecking your photograph.*"

"Not funny. Not funny at all."

Since the advent of digital picture-taking rather than film, photobombing has become more popular. Some of the more famous photobombers are President Clinton, Anna Pavlova, a stingray and a squirrel.[53]

Now you will definitely win any bet that challenges you to name what Clinton, Pavlova, stingray, and squirrel all have in common.

The answer: "These four have never been to one of my pool parties." Except for the stingray of course.

A bomb makes a boom, making it slightly *onomatopoeic*, a word whose pronunciation echoes its action, the way the word *snap* snaps, *tick* ticks, and *bomb* booms. Boom! We just blew up your photo.

The trick is on you, you two photo-boomers.

Your background high jinks made the shot even better.

*The unexpected thing that appears without warning.* You don't know what you've shot until, back home, you begin loading the camera card to your computer.

Not that Meg didn't know about those two jokers in the background. She was well aware of them, but she remained unaware of just how they might appear.

She ended up very pleasantly surprised.

To their everlasting dismay.

How happy the photo-bomber appears in the field of view! Petals a-tremble, stamen extending, pistils a-twinkle, sepals seeping.

Celebrating the spoils.

Shaking the booty.

Bombing in the background.

I think it's best to leave them in that state of ecstasy. Who needs to tell them that, when it comes to wrecking photos, they've bombed.

This photo asks you to drop some photobombs on your unsuspecting family and friends and followers.

Be the bomb in the background or the one taking the shot who is pretending not to notice the others' attempts to mess up your moment.

Rather than steal all the attention, maybe that background bomb gives your foreground figure its pop!

And if indeed the photobomb creates pop, well then you're livin' the onomatopoeic, ironic dream, just like Clinton, Pavlova, Stingray, and Squirrel.

Go you.

Here's some odd information from Grammarist:

# 18: ENTER A CHAOTIC ZONE

"All tales," writes John Yorke, "are at some level a journey into the woods to find the missing part of us, to retrieve it and make ourselves whole."[54]

"Beyond [the known world]," writes Joseph Campbell, "is darkness, the unknown, and danger; just as beyond the parental watch is danger to the infant and beyond the protection of his society danger to the member of the tribe."[55] He continues, "The adventure is always and everywhere a passage beyond the veil of the known into the unknown; the powers that watch at the boundary are dangerous; to deal with them is risky; yet for anyone with competence and courage the danger fades."[56]

Competence and courage. Oh, that's all it takes to make the danger fade?

I'm in deep trouble.

Outside the cave in the photo, the hieroglyphic-shadows demand our attention. "Abandon all hope, ye who enter here" warns Dante's gate of Hell. This cave, we hope, says something a bit more welcoming. Leaves connote both growth and decay, danger and hope. As with most journeys into the beyond, the message at the beginning is mixed.

The "cave drawings" might be ferns: Earth first saw ferns about 360 million years ago; they appeared before the dinosaurs roamed the sky and land. As symbols, "ferns were seen as good luck, often for new lovers. The fern symbolizes eternal youth."[57]

In myths and stories, chaotic zones take many forms: Darkness, The Jungle, Mountains, The Unknown, The Watery Abyss, Madness, The Cosmic Night, Deep Forests, The Desert, The Underworld, Caves, The Void, The Belly of the Beast, Battlefields.

In leaving our known world, we return to a child-like state, trembling at the threshold between our safe beds and the dark closet.

That closet contains something precious, something we've put away and forgotten on that upper shelf, gathering dust.

Something missing.

A part.

Of ourselves.

For four years, from 1999 - 2003, practically twenty-four hours a day, I experienced undiagnosed panic attacks—in front of a class I was teaching, sitting at a table in a restaurant, asleep in the middle of the night. Everything inside raced, an endless flutter, trying to beat its way out, pounding in my chest, my head, all my limbs trembling and afire. No place became safe. At the end, I ended up pretty much unable to go anywhere, confined to a single room in the house. I know: so Emily Dickinson of me.

Long story short: a diagnosis and therapy brought me back, but not to my old self.

A new self was born!

I began writing.

Again.

As I did when I was young, when writing was a new love, seemingly millions of years ago.

Eternal youth. Many a journey into chaos has begun with that desire—to both recover our young selves and to lose our old ones. In youth, we were all dreams and potential, projecting our desires into some fantastical future. And now?

We are still those youngsters. Still those dreams. Still mad to live, burning to become.

The cave and its welcoming "cave-writings" from ancient ferns, perhaps, ask you this week to find your youth again, remind you that you hid it away somewhere, some place in the dark, but it's eternally yours, eternally there, eternally waiting for you to go back, into the woods, to recover.

# 19: CALL OUT AN OXYMORON

*xymoron*: the marriage of two opposites. Some famous ones include: *jumbo shrimp, bittersweet, definitely maybe*.

This image might be a visual oxymoron. Or close to one. Meg calls it "Pink Army."

Bloom and Bloom discuss the attraction of opposites for *Psychology Today*:

Opposites, or perhaps more accurately, 'complements' do attract. Introverts and extroverts, morning people and night people, impulsives and planners, steady plodders and adrenaline junkies, adventure-grabbers and security-seekers…[58]

Putting opposites side-by-side immediately creates tension and power:

When Marcel Duchamp placed…a urinal in an art gallery and called it *Fountain* he was simply extrapolating this process—making the gallery itself the frame of the work. *The Fountain's* power grows from its environment; from the fact it simply doesn't belong. Two opposites are placed side by side; art is rendered from juxtaposition. That interpretation is the art…When the shapes coalesce and evoke a truth from their association, the observer is rewarded with an overwhelmingly powerful experience.[59]

so much depends
upon

a red wheel
barrow

glazed with rain
water

beside the white
chickens

"The Red Wheelbarrow"
William Carlos William

Juxtaposition: the words are both next to each other and separated, like *wheel* from *barrow*, *rain* from *water*. The "glazed" implies the arrival of the sun after a rain, that light drawing out the white chickens, bringing together what the storm had separated.

Is the human-made barrow in the midst of all this nature like a urinal in a gallery, the thing that doesn't seem to belong? Are the human-made words at odds with the world itself and its word-less Nature? Are we ourselves trapped in an oxymoron: Human Nature?

The poem could keep going, juxtaposition after juxtaposition, one thing beside another, each one changing the moment, the meaning, each association rewarding us as they coalesce into a whole.

So the world keeps changing, evolving, one thing next to another, like the Big Bang, our world originating in something infinitesimally tiny, a concentrated nothingness.

Out of these contradictions, out of this marriage of opposites, meaning explodes onto the scene, ever-expanding.

This week, the Pink Army wants you, you oxymoron, you.

Recruit more oxymorons for the cause.
Juxtapose opposites.
Find things that don't belong together.

Do it as if so much depends upon it.
Because it does.

# 20: MARRY TWO UN-OPPOSITES

The previous message—to marry two opposites—finds here its own opposite: the marriage of like-mindedness.

Birds of a feather, as they say, flock together. Like two peas in a pod.

Let me tell you about Meg, our invisible photographer and the love of my life.

We met at the ripe old age of 23 when she came to my Chicago apartment with her friend, who was dating one of my roommates.

"There you are!" we both seemed to say. "I've been waiting so very long to meet you."

She laughed freely, shone with a natural, classic beauty, spoke with a fierce intelligence, and brimmed with wondrous, childlike playfulness.

After our first official date six months later (it took me a few months to get over the fear that I would somehow blow it all), she said, "Don't disappear."

I took that message to heart, still here, over thirty years later.

The image of two peas in a pod, of soul mates, of two that create one also has special powers, also works to create magic. If you are lucky enough to meet your soul mate, well, there are signs.

According to Kelsey Borresen, these include the following:[60]

1. You communicate without speaking.
2. You know in your gut that you've found The One.
3. The physical chemistry is palpable.
4. You've been totally comfortable around each other since day one.
5. But the relationship isn't all rainbows and butterflies. He or she challenges you like no one else can.
6. You may not see eye-to-eye on every little thing, but you're on the same page where it really matters.
7. The relationship brings both partners a sense of inner calm.
8. You and your partner have separate identities, but you face the world as one.
9. You may have known each other for years, but you suddenly find yourselves ready for love at the same time.

Clearly, these two flowers have all that. How ready for love are they? And that physical chemistry! Come on, you two! Get a room.

Twin flames. Heart's desire. Kindred spirit. True love. Helpmate. Love matched with love, the one "pillow'd upon [a] fair love's ripening breast/ to feel for ever its soft fall and swell."[61]

The imagery of "peas in a pod" inspires us, leads us from the ephemeral to the infinite, from the moment to always.

Till a' the seas gang dry, my dear,
And the rocks melt wi' the sun;
I will love thee still, my dear,
While the sands o' life shall run.

And fare thee weel, my only luve!
And fare thee weel awhile!
And I will come again, my luve,
Though it were ten thousand mile.[62]

Perhaps, metaphor—"Juliet is the sun"—is a practical way "we contrive to talk about two things at once; two…subject matters are mingled to rich and unpredictable effect." And, in doing so, we suggest "something inherently complex, open-ended, and resistant to compact literal statement."[63]

This week, consider, rather than marrying opposites, playing a game of mingling and mixing complementary terms.

Begin with the simple seed sentence *X is Y*—and see how quickly this marriage of like-mindedness blossoms into unpredictable, rich effects.

# 21: WATCH YOUR BACK

*P*aranoia is what they'll call it if you think they're out to get you, if you think your back needs to be watched. "They're out there," begins Ken Kesey's *One Flew Over the Cuckoo's Nest*, a seriously paranoid statement if I ever heard one.

Unless of course, they really are out there, yes?

Then, it would be sheer insanity *not* to watch your back.

"If they can get you asking the wrong questions, they don't have to worry about answers."
—Thomas Pynchon, *Gravity's Rainbow*

"Panic is the sudden realization that everything around you is alive."
—William S. Burroughs, *Ghost of Chance*

"Strange how paranoia can link up with reality now and then."
—Philip K. Dick, *A Scanner Darkly*

"Just because you're paranoid doesn't mean they aren't after you."
—Joseph Heller, *Catch-22*

In the photo, notice the slow curve of the back, that openness, that vulnerability.

As in horror films, the audience shouts: "Turn around! Turn around!"

For Goodness sake, watch your back.

There's something implied about being told to "watch your back," isn't there? Something to do with being careful about what you say because there might be consequences.

Like a knife in the back.

Ouch.

If you spend all your time watching your back, though, you might miss what's in front of you. That can wreak havoc on your nose.

Atlas once led the rebellion to topple the heavens, only to be condemned to hold the heavens in place (not Earth as is often pictured). He stands in the gardens of the nymphs of the sunset, known as the Hesperides; they just happened also to be Atlas' three daughters.

Upon his shoulders, supported by his back, Atlas endures the weight of the celestial spheres, the sky and all that lies beyond.

Without Atlas' enduring back, the sky falls upon us, covering us in cosmic ruins.

Perhaps that is what will bring about the end of the world.

Atlas' back gives out.

Maybe we better watch *his* back!

What is it like when someone doesn't have your back? Shauna H Springer Ph.D. lists these signs:

- When you feel like your partner doesn't respect or like you very much.
- When you feel like your partner will assume the worst about you.
- When you feel like your partner is looking for ways that you will screw up or let them down.
- When your partner is rude, hostile, or detached (in the latter case, signaling possible rejection).[64]

Not to sound too paranoid, but they're out there, and maybe it isn't just your own back they're after.

This week, have your partner's back.

This week, know they're out there.

Fight back against "them" with respect, support, and belief. Assume the best in your partner. Fight back with compassion, attachment, and interest.

And while you're watching your partner's back, your partner will have yours.

# 22: UNSTRING THE STRUNG OUT

"All objects in our universe," according to string theory, "are composed of vibrating filaments (strings) and membranes (branes) of energy."[65]

Makes me wonder who strung the instrument and what He, She, They, or It has been playing all this time.

Please, please, please don't be "It's a Small World." Please.

A universe of strings and branes. Strings & Branes. I think I saw that band in college: a bunch of Ph.D. students on mandolins.

If you find a watch, the argument goes, then there must be a watchmaker. Finding a design to the universe also implies a designer, the one who made it so. In Robert Frost's "Design," the poem's speaker comes across a design: a dimpled spider, fat and white, on a white heal-all flower holding up a white moth. The speaker, in the second stanza, asks: "What had that flower to do with being white, / The wayside blue and innocent heal-all? / What brought the kindred spider to that height, / Then steered the white moth thither in the night?" Yes, a design, but maybe a design to "appall, if design govern in a thing so small." Of the ending, Andrew Spacey has this analysis:

The final question suggests that this design is dark in nature, intended to appall, that is, shock and nauseate. Note that appall has as its root a Latin word which means 'to pale.' Frost must have chosen this word to further complicate proceedings. The final line then brings uncertainty but the word 'govern' implies that there is a power in charge somehow, in some way, pulling the strings.[66]

Ah, pulling the strings, not plucking them. Like those finger string games, cat's cradle wasn't it? Frost wonders if the designer indeed plays for our amusement or for the designer's own darker delight. In something so small does the designer take notice, play a part, pluck a string?

Strings have different vibrational states, a string's properties at any given moment determined by the different ways it can vibrate. The tones of a stringed instrument are determined by the length, tension, and thickness of the string.

The Designer is the world's most gifted guitarist. Or harpist. Or mandolinist. Or maybe the Designer plays a whole stringed orchestra.

Imagine that playlist.

Odd note: the song that works for any playlist is "Heaven is a Place on Earth."

They say in heaven love comes first.

Surrounding and serenading us everlastingly, strings play their symphonies, their harmonies, their discordant notes.

Or is it more like that kids' cat's cradle game, an intricate web that, with one wrong pull, all falls apart around us?

No wonder we're all strung out. The playing never ends: the plucking, the pulling, our branes overstuffed, our strings on their last nerve.

This week, listen to the strings playing and let them inspire you to design your own playlist. Try for 80 minutes of music that you've forgotten. Each song will be a strand of your own universal "good vibrations."

And, for god's sake, no "Who Let the Dogs Out?" Woof, woof, woof, woof, woof.

(And yes, you can curse me later for putting that song in our branes.)

# 23: TIME TO TAKE UP TINKING

In the world of knitting, a UFO is defined as such:

**U.F.O.**: *Unfinished object*. Some projects are destined to be UFOs forever, lying around half-knitted until you finally decide to frog them.

**Frogging**: Giving up on a project and ripping out the stitches. So named because the sound it makes, supposedly, is 'rip-it rip-it rip-it.'[67]

This image conjures up, for me, that sense of knitting, the droplets of water emphasizing the knitted covering's protective qualities.

This plant's going to be okay.

It went outside with its jacket on.

In fact, not being able to make a proper coat might've killed the Neanderthals:

There is archaeological evidence to suggest that humans had better technology for making their garments. We had already developed specialised cutting tools, like blades and eventually needles. These helped us cut animal hide in shapes like rectangles and squares, which could then be joined together. In contrast, Neanderthals seem only to have had simple scrapers. In 2007, Gilligan proposed that this contributed to their downfall, by leaving them with lower-quality clothes during the coldest periods of the last ice age.[68]

The good people at Wool & the Gang tell us to take up *tinking*.

Un-knitting or tinking is a great skill for any knitter to have, possibly one of the most useful skills in fact. This technique allows you to move backwards a few stitches to fix a mistake or correct a stitch—which can happen to anyone.[69]

Knit backwards.
Tink.

Want to be the hit at the knit party? Open with this line: "I had to frog UFO after UFO until I took up tinking."

From the working needle to the main needle, you pull the stitch, undoing, unknitting, unmaking.
Tinking.
What's done cannot be undone.
Except by tinking.

Because she's so small, Tinkerbell can only feel one emotion at a time.

In the novel, after Wendy leaves Neverland, Tink dies.

And Peter no longer remembers her.

The Tinkerbell effect "describes things that are thought to exist only because people believe in them." To bring Tinkerbell into existence, kids bring their hands together, as in knitting, bringing something magical into existence. The Tinkerbell effect implies that "with the overwhelming amount of sensory information, the brain summarizes it by filling in what it cannot make sense of. In other words, it is an act of imagination."[70]

This week, tink about the UFOs you've forgotten about—and return not to knit them together but to un-knit, to unstitch.

Tink about the Neanderthals, extinkt because they didn't tear up the old and retool.

Unloop.

Unconnect.

Toaday, tink instead of frog.

Instead of rip-it, rip-it, rip-it, tink it.

# 24: EXPERIMENT WITH CHEMISTRY

*A*toms, we know, cannot be trusted. They make up everything.

When atoms find they have a special connection, they bond into molecules.

Chemistry.

Symptoms that you've found chemistry:

1. You have easy banter.
2. You get each other's sense of humor.
3. You are immediately comfortable.
4. You can just be yourself.
5. It just flows naturally.[71]

According to Kelly Campbell, the core components of both friendship and romantic chemistry include these:

- non-judgment
- similarity
- mystery
- attraction
- mutual trust
- effortless communication

Also, she found people were more likely to experience friendship chemistry if their personalities were…

- …open (e.g., adventurous, imaginative, and emotionally in-tune)
- …conscientious (e.g., competent, disciplined, hard-working)
- …agreeable (e.g., friendly, cooperative, and considerate)[72]

Atoms are so numerous that…we'd find that approximately one atom in everyone's lungs, at any moment, was in Caesar's (or Lenin's, or George Washington's, or Alexandre Dumas') lungs as they exhaled their final breath.[73]

Or Sojourner Truth's.
Or Marie Curie's.
Or Rosa Parks'.
Or Amelia Earhart's.

Chemistry focuses on matter, on the how and why of combinations, separations, formations, reactions. Chemistry connects everyone and everything in the universe.

All who exist. All who Argon.

This week, create some chemistry between you and the world. I've noticed how Meg approaches each photo shoot: with that sense of imaginative openness, conscientious discipline, and cooperative consideration.

Be open and agreeable to what you might encounter.

Approach without judgment.
Start up an easy conversation.
Look for similarities, connections.
Notice, too, the mysterious aspects.
Feel the attraction.
Trust the moment.

Breathe in the molecules of the first and last breaths of everyone who has ever lived.

Feel the connection.
Feel the mystery.
The chemistry.

# 25: FIND THE WIDOWED OBJECT

*O*bjects return, in dreams, in words, in pictures, haunting us. Ghost-like hallucinations from a drug trip, they demand our immediate attention—not just for that one time, but forever, always on the verge of returning.

A 2011 study of 2,679 regular hallucinogen users in Drug and Alcohol Dependence found that 60.6 percent had experienced hallucinations reminiscent of trips while they were sober. Common visual distortions experienced during flashbacks include perceiving objects as larger or smaller than they are, seeing lines trailing off objects, and noticing something looming at the edge of your vision.[74]

We go on a trip—and it is the trip that later returns to us, larger, smaller, trailing off, looming.

Charles Baxter introduces us to "the concept of defamiliarization, which means to make the familiar strange, and the strange familiar," a concept he connects to Gerald Hopkins' "nature of the obsessive image, the 'widowed' image, the image that sticks in the memory as if glued there." He continues here:

Hopkins appeared to believe that images became memorable when some crucial part of their meaning had been stripped from them. Sometimes an obsessive image is the product of a trauma. The trauma cannot be remembered but has left its trace in misfit details. You may not remember your violent abusive uncle very well, but his blue glass ashtray or his decoy duck stays in your memory as if riveted there. The burden of the feeling is taken on by the objects. Shock is registered through these objects but the origin of the shock is protected. The objects, as a consequence, have a feeling of impatience and scale, as a fetish does. Hopkins describes these obsessive images of objects as things for which he has not 'found the law.' They are unfulfilled in meaning, but they take up a lot of room in the memory as if in compensation. They seem both gratuitous and inexplicably necessary.[75]

Inexplicably necessary. The image returns to us, filling but unfulfilled. We see it in the blur, in the corners of our vision, other times in clear focus, in every inkblot the world throws at us.

Why, the man asks the psychiatrist, do you keep showing me pictures of [  ]? What fills in that blank for you? What picture keeps popping like a widowed wing, demanding your attention?

*widow.* **figurative**. To deprive of something essential, important, or highly valued; to bereave; to dispossess.[76]

The possessed object points to dispossession, the loss of something essential. For us to grow up, we must destroy our childhoods.

In gaining our adulthoods, what did we widow?

What did we lose?

What must we recover?

This week, look upon the image and see what returns to you. Reflect upon those objects you see that seem beyond the law, appearing whenever and wherever they choose, haunting. Think of your own widowed images, the ones that appeared to have died long ago but keep rising, undead, unfulfilled, unrelenting.

Think, too, of the concept of defamiliarization. Think of taking something familiar to us and making it strangely unfamiliar.

Take a trip into the trip that keeps returning to you.

What looms at its edges?

What misfit details call you back to the island that is, perhaps, your long lost home?

# 26: CHOOSE BETWEEN NEW & OLD

alfway.
Another threshold to cross.
The point of no return.
Hold hands. Hold tight.
Here we go.

In stories, according to John Yorke, the midpoint is the moment something profoundly significant occurs; the midpoint marks a massive escalation in jeopardy, and it raises the stakes. There can be no return to how life was before.

It's the point at which, in the 'Hero's Journey', the protagonist enters the 'enemy cave' and steals the 'elixir'; it is—in our paradigm—the moment of 'big change'. It isn't necessarily the most dramatic moment, but it is a point of supreme significance. As *Macbeth* illustrates, it's the point from which there's no going back. A new 'truth' dawns on our hero for the first time; the protagonist has captured the treasure or found the 'elixir' to heal their flaw. But there's an important caveat … At this stage in the story they don't quite know how to handle it correctly. The 'journey back' is therefore built on how the hero reacts to possessing the 'elixir' and whether they will learn to master it in a wise and useful way.[77]

Here, you face a choice: move forward by calling on lessons you have learned or return to your old self.

If you choose to move forward, one warning. There's no going back.

You've sensed the elixir, not only one that might cure *you*, but one that also has the power to cure the wasted world, the power to bring a new vision to the same-old, same-old.

Will you listen to that voice in your head?

Imagine it's that young girl with the backpack, seeing a glimpse of a new world, while at the same time her current world holds her tight.

An Emersonian voice from the portal: "Whoso would be [fully human] must be a nonconformist."

But school, the tennis team—they all are rewarding her for playing by the rules, for conforming, for stepping into the pre-defined roles and playing her part.

Yet she sees with a growing awareness the holes in their world, the cracks, the way each step into their world takes her away from her own ideas of girls, of women, of Self, of right and wrong.

That hand of a parent holds her, a hand that has always accepted her the way she is, was, will be. How can she let that go?

How can she join a world that is so phony?

How can she reject it and give up those other hands waiting to hold her in place?

This new world calls. It is a tricky world, a world where one must balance the desires of the Self with the demands of the Society.

Can she let go of that hand that holds her to the old world, a world where she could stay forever young, forever attached? Why would she ever ever want to let go?

Because she must.

Otherwise, she's forever stagnant, forever chained, forever un-growing.

So she must let go if she is to become herself.

This week, step up to a threshold that seems to be asking you to decide between hanging onto an old belief system and a dawning new one.

What would mean a point of no return?

You see yourself as a photographer, but you haven't yet bought a camera. The money in savings that you're holding onto is for something else, yes? More of the same? Or for that camera you've been eyeing at The Camera Shop?

You see yourself taking your shot.

You see those old roles, that borrowed sense of Self clinging to you.

Another shot. Another one.

Another tug at your heartstrings.

This week, buy that camera.

# 27: READ YOUR EGGS

Some eggs for your Sunday morning brunch? Oomancy, divination by eggs, was once widespread.

According to Rachel Warren Chadd, "The white (albumen) of the egg would be dropped into water and various predictions would be made according to the shapes it formed."[78] In fact, Elizabeth Parris and Abigail Williams were just some of the girls of Salem who practiced reading omens using an egg and a mirror ("Venus glass").

"There's a patch of old snow in a corner," writes Robert Frost, "That I should have guessed / Was a blow-away paper the rain / Had brought to rest." He is perhaps asking us to "read" Nature, if not for divination, at least for the news of the day.

I'm working on a collection of prose poems about the world without us, after we've drowned because we couldn't read Nature.

**But It's Hard to Let Go**

The caretakers have taken their leave. The wardens deserted the windows and doors unlatched into the wobbly world. This fresh suburban sprawl—the McWilds, the McWoods, the twittering blue-bloods. A spider-spun veil covers strewn limbs, marries the path once connecting company to the rebuffed borders. Next door, on the cobwebbed trellis, the crowning rosebushes complete their public careers. A stonewall counts its modern decay rock by rock, a peculiar new glory. In the oak's crooked bough, a plastic Easter egg totters; inside, a seed somersaults. The pod's trap door springs like a time limit, summoning the final stage—larva, pupa, moth. The sky cracks open; the moth flutters against its outskirts, toward the snow lightning: a sleigh, a basket, the terrible present wow.

In a possible future, spider-webs cover our paths, the manicured gardens now grown wild; our walls fall rock by rock, and out of a pupae left in a plastic Easter Egg, a moth flies toward a Christmas sky, without us.

Whether you poach, soft-boil, hard-boil, scramble, omelet, fritatta, over easy, over hard, over Goldilocks-style, hash, bake or baste them, your eggs need your eyes, your interpretation, your ability to turn what they are into something else, a sign of the times to come.

In Tristan Dooley's *How to Read Nature*, he suggests the following as a start:

Go for a three-minute walk outdoors. Note down the things your eyes are drawn toward. If we have an understanding of the things our brain is likely to prioritize, then we can temporarily override this pecking order and we will start to see new things.[79]

"Some people are weatherwise," wrote Benjamin Franklin, "but most are otherwise."

Nature tells us we can no longer be otherwise.

It's time to take note.

This week, go ahead: start taking note of nature.

Read your eggs, your gardens, that pile of rain in the corner.

Capture, in some form, the message that you are hearing loud and clear.

Be the translator.

Send it back at us.

Before it's too late.

TRAPPED BLOSSOM   66

# 28: FREE THE INNOCENT

*W*hat was this flower's crime?

Close your eyes.

Imagine a world where just being a flower is the crime.

Now open them.

And here you are.

In the summer of 2018, came this report from AP News:

Inside an old warehouse in South Texas, hundreds of children wait in a series of cages created by metal fencing. One cage had 20 children inside. Scattered about are bottles of water, bags of chips and large foil sheets intended to serve as blankets.[80]

*Those who cannot remember the past are condemned to repeat it.*
— George Santayana

'Evil' has become the word we apply to perpetrators who we're both unable and unwilling to do anything to repair, and for whom all of our mechanisms of justice seem unequal: it describes the limits of what malevolence we're able to bear. In the end, it's a word that says more about the helplessness of the accuser than it does the transgressor. As [Peter] Dews writes, 'Basic notions of offence and punishment, of transgression and forgiveness, seem to lose their grip in the face of profound, far reaching desecrations of the human.' For those kinds of crimes, 'evil' is still the only word we've got.[81]

From *The American Civil Liberties Union*, update on class action lawsuit, 2018:

The government has since provided the court with data that indicates at least 2,654 immigrant children were separated from their parents or caregivers as a result of Trump administration policies.[82]

I think of the Little Prince and his desire to protect the flower on his planet. I think of the sheep and the flower's vulnerability.

Through the lattice, in the photo, we glimpse the flower, the juxtaposition of the hard iron emphasizing the flower's fragility.

One can imagine that, like the glass around the Little Prince's flower, the cage protects.

One might hope for such a world.

Might one?

Despite the confusion of the philosophers, the word 'evil' is still in common use. [Susan] Neiman herself is understandably reluctant to offer a single, narrow definition of her own for what 'evil' means today, but what she does suggest is a useful description of what effect evil has. 'Calling something 'evil,' she writes [in the 2002 book *Evil in Modern Thought*], 'is a way of marking the fact that it shatters our trust in the world.' Evil is both harmful and inexplicable, but not just that; what defines an evil act is that it is permanently disorienting for all those touched by it.[83]

This week, consider what 'evil' means in today's world. What does it look like?

Look up at the sky. Ask yourself, "Has the sheep eaten the flower or not?" And you'll see how everything changes. . . .

# 29: BELIEVE IN THE FORCE

*I'*m back at the amusement park, my back pushed against the wall panels, lights flashing, music blaring.

My flip-flops fall to the—oh my God, the floor isn't there!

Not only am I going to throw-up, but for the rest of the time at the park, I'm going to be barefoot.

The ride is completely enclosed, with 48 padded panels lining the inside wall. Riders lean against these panels, which are angled back. As the ride rotates, centrifugal force is exerted against the pads by the rider, removing the rider from the floor, due to the slant…. The riders are experiencing centrifugal force equivalent to three times the force of gravity.[84]

The Gravitron. That's what made me understand that maybe I wasn't suited to be an astronaut.

Here, in this photograph, the red riders spin against the yellow walls. Physics folks argue over whether centrifugal force even exists, a fictitious force some call it, more the result of centripedal force and inertia.

All I know is what I feel.
Back pressed against the wall.

Floor disappearing.
Something presses against me.
Something holds me there.

A hand, perhaps. An old leathered hand. Force seen as an invisible hand: pushing things back to earth, the push of a magnet, a hand squishing atoms together, another one gradually pulling them apart. A push. A pull. Something that happens between one thing and another.

Force. The hand that pulled the lever, started the flowers spinning.

Force. The attraction that drew our photographer Meg to this flower's center.

Use the Force.

Creative force, like a musical composer, goes on unwearyingly repeating a simple air or theme, now high, now low, in solo, in chorus, ten thousand times reverberated, till it fills earth and heaven with the chant.
—Ralph Waldo Emerson[85]

**force of nature**

1. Literally, the earth's powerful climatological phenomena, such as wind or rain, that humans cannot control.
2. Someone or something with a huge and seemingly unstoppable amount of energy, influence, or force.[86]

This week, imagine being able to see the invisible forces that push and pull, bind and unbind.

What forces your back against the wall, holding you in place while the floor falls away?

What spins you 'round, 'round, like a record, baby?

In *Star Wars*, the Force is the invisible glue holding together a fragmentary, broken universe.

"The Force," Obi-Wan Kenobi tells us, "is what gives Jedi [their] power. It's an energy field created by all living things. It surrounds us and penetrates us. It binds the galaxy together."

Feel the Force.
But don't force it.
Or the force just might spin off in a different direction.
What does it look like? Feel like?

# 30: EXPRESS A QUALITY APART

**abstract**
- expressing a quality apart from an object
- having only intrinsic form with little or no attempt at pictorial representation or narrative content[87]

One might think of abstract as capturing the spirit of a thing rather than the thing itself. To "abstract" is to detach, disengage, uncouple. There's an attempt to transcend, a movement away from the earth, a movement toward the clouds.

*Concrete* stands as abstract's opposite. With concrete, we build, solidify. According to dream analysts,

To dream of concrete represents ideas, plans, or situations that are permanent. A solid foundation or absolutely knowing that something in your life can't fail. An area of your life where there is absolute certainty. Confidence in a situation or relationship that doesn't go away.[88]

Is there something unconfident, unpermanent, uncertain about the abstract? To embrace the abstract, must we cuddle with uncertainty?

Abstraction, according to the editors at Phaidon, "rejects representation and any relationship to the natural world."[89] What do we make of this new abstraction as seen in Meg's photograph(s), one that celebrates the natural world?—that sees within that world the chance to peek inside, to peek beyond, as if looking into the dreams of its designer?

To "abstract" nature is perhaps to remove it from our preconceived notions, to have us see it anew, to wonder once more at its essential inscrutability.

To see past its poker face, to see the hand it holds. Likely, a royal flush.

"We look at the world once, in childhood," writes Louise Gluck. "The rest is memory."

Perhaps abstraction erases the memory, returns us to that first glimpse.

In Ancient Greece, "Mnemosyne was the Titan goddess of memory and remembrance, and the inventress of language and words, the mother of the nine muses."[90]

It is she, perhaps, who first imagined poetry, a weaving together of memory and words, a way for us to take control of time, ticking like a bomb we cannot defuse.

With abstraction, we can remove ourselves from the situation, see another way out.

"With the invention of photography," writes John Berger, "we acquired a new means of expression more closely associated with memory than any other. The Muse of photography is not one of Memory's daughter, but Memory herself."[91]

In photograph after photograph here in this book and elsewhere, it is we who are removed, returned to a time when we didn't know what we were looking it.

This week's image invites you on that journey into nature without guidebooks.

Make no attempt to place what you see into a story with the handed-down words and labels from your past.

Remove it petal by petal from what you know. See something new form.

Look at it at once, as in childhood.

The rest is memory.

# 31: REDISCOVER FROST

Of course, you've heard about the road not taken, perhaps Frost's most famous and misunderstood verse. In the poem, believe it or not, the two roads "equally lay," no discernible difference between them except later, when the speaker recounts his choice to take the "less traveled one." The difference in one's life made by taking one road over another is all in the speaker's mind, in the re-telling, in the desire to give meaning to our choices.

Frost rewards re-reading.

To read or re-read Robert Frost is to enter a world of play. "Mending Wall" begins with the idea that there's something that doesn't love a wall, "that sends the frozen-ground-swell under it." The frozen-ground-swell? Isn't that frost? Did he just make a pun on his own name?

Or this line that appears later in the poem: "Before I built a wall I'd ask to know / what I was walling in or walling out, / and to whom I was like to give offense." Give "a fence"! How fun!

His "Once by the Pacific" begins, "The shattered water made a misty din." Shouldn't *misty* describe *water*—and *shattered* describe *din*. Did he just mix up our senses? He just laid some synesthesia on us.

In "Birches," the speaker, a swinger-of-birches, vacillates between heaven and Earth, at one point deciding, "Earth's the right place for love: / I don't know where it's likely to go better."

Things point to heaven in Frost's world—ladders, trees, a boy on a birch—as if reaching for the sky before it fell, the world without its limitations, without death and decay and its continual sinking, sinking toward grief.

But Earth's the right place, the only place one might argue, for love.

The ending of "Stopping by Woods on a Snowy Evening" might have the ring of familiarity for readers:

The woods are lovely, dark and deep,
But I have promises to keep,
And miles to go before I sleep,
And miles to go before I sleep.

Before this moment, the speaker wonders "whose woods these are, I think I know." Now he wonders at their un-knowability, their resistance to human ideas of ownership, farmhouses, villages. To rediscover Frost is to rediscover the natural world, rich with all the meanings, metaphors, and allegories we've attached to it, a symbiosis of sorts, a coupling.

In another poem, within a well-curb, the poet's speaker glimpses "a something white, uncertain, / something more of the depths." Along comes a ripple: "Blurred it, blotted it out. What was that whiteness? / Truth? A pebble of quartz? For once, then, something."

Frost doesn't know. He asks questions but doesn't play God by making up answers.

This image of frost asks you to wake up today to Frost.

In "The Oven Bird," "the question that he frames in all but words / is what to make of a diminished thing."

Another question.

*Diminish.*
To make smaller, lessen, reduce in size.
Is that what poems do?
What frost does?
For this week, of the world and for the world, make a diminished thing.
Not as an answer.
But as a question for us all.

# 32: LIVE THE WITCH'S LIFE

Out of the bokeh-blur, Meg in this photograph creates a vase for her flowers.

Like magic.

Maybe, although my heart is a kitten of butter,
I am blowing it up like a zeppelin.
Yes. It is the witch's life.
—Anne Sexton

A vase of bokeh. A kitten of butter. Such is the witch's life, a life of transformations, familiars, visions, recipes, eye of newt, filet of fenny-snake.

Cauldron's root is the Latin *caldarium*, meaning hot-bath. The phlox flowers in the vase derive from the Greek φλέγειν, to burn.

The town does not exist / except where one black-haired tree slips / up like a drowned woman into / the hot sky. / The town is silent. The night / boils with eleven stars. / Oh starry night!
—Anne Sexton

Madness. From 1300-1850, 6,887 in Germany; 5,691 in Switzerland; 1,663 in France; 474 in Hungary; 378 in Belgium; 367 in England; 280 in Norway; 190 in Scotland; 115 in Finland; and

99 in Luxembourg: witch-trials ending in death.[92]

To be a witch is to burn.

Of photography, National Geographic Magazine's Joel Sartore writes the following:

Composition and seeing well is really the heart of [photography]. All successful images are composed so that different elements in a photograph come together to tell a story. Composition involves looking and thinking and then deciding what it is you want to say with your pictures, and it is one way of making order out of the chaos of life. Composition really is the hardest thing… out of everything to master.[93]

Witches see things—something wicked this way comes—that the rest of us lack the vision to discern. Where we see s, witches see kittens of butter blowing up like zeppelins. Their sky boils with stars. Out of nothing, they form a purple vase for their phloxes.

Looking and thinking deeply, witches reinvent themselves and the world. What the world doesn't provide, they summon; what powers the world hides from them, they call upon. They compose. They

see. They engage in the hardest thing to master: turning the world's madness into sense.

I have ridden in your cart, driver, / waved my nude arms at villages going by, / learning the last bright routes, survivor where your flames still bite my thigh / and my ribs crack where your wheels wind. / A woman like that is not ashamed to die. / I have been her kind.
—Anne Sexton

The human race is a very, very magical race. We have a magic power of witches and wizards. We're here on this earth to unravel the mystery of this planet. The planet is asking for it.
—Yoko Ono

I think that there is incredible prejudice about witches while there is no prejudice about wizards. Words are very important, and I'm really into destroying myths.
—Yoko Ono[94]

This week, call upon your inner witch.
Cast your spells.
Summon your deeper powers.
Compose the constituents.
Fill your heart until it blows.

# 33: FLOAT LIKE ALI

*I*n the signed postcard I have from Muhammad Ali, he drew a picture of a boxing ring, then wrote *The Greatest of All Times*.

With a smiley face.

*Float like a butterfly, sting like a bee. The hands can't hit what the eyes can't see.*

I once rewrote Allen Ginsberg's "America" and added to his verses, the additions in blue:

America when I was seven mamma took me to Unitarian Universalist meetings they sold us garbanzos a handful per ticket a ticket costs a nickel and the speeches were free everybody was angelic and spiritual about the world it was all so sincere you have no idea what a good thing the practice was in 1972 the minister a grand old boxing fan a real mensch, a fighter too, we watched Muhammad Ali in the church basement, every beautiful word made me cry: 'I am America. I am the part you won't recognize. But you get used to me—black, confident, cocky; my name, not yours; my religion, not yours; my goals, my own. Get used to me.' I knew everyone in every church must love him just as I did.

My father loved Muhammad Ali. I once asked him why, but I can't remember his answer. I imagine it had something to do with Ali's not being all show. He dreamed big, but backed it up just as big.

*The man who has no imagination has no wings.*

I too loved—love—Ali. I still think about him almost every day. I wonder how someone grows into a superhero; I wonder at such strength of character. The Greatest.

*I don't have to be what you want me to be.*

Ali died in 2016.

Between April 2017 and April 2018, beekeepers in the U.S. lost an estimated 40 percent of their managed honey bee colonies, according to an annual survey conducted by the Bee Informed Partnership.[95]

*I should be a postage stamp, because that's the only way I'll ever get licked. I'm beautiful. I'm fast. I'm so mean I make medicine sick. I can't possibly be beat.*

He stood for something disappearing from the world. GOAT. Greatest of all times.

*I got no quarrel with them Vietcong.*

His spirit inspires me daily.

*Impossible is just a big word thrown around by small men who find it easier to live in the world they've been given than to explore the power they have to change it. Impossible is not a fact. It's an opinion. Impossible is not a declaration. It's a dare. Impossible is potential. Impossible is temporary. Impossible is nothing.*

This week, be inspired by the man who floats like butterflies, stings like a bee.

*Braggin' is when a person says something and can't do it. I do what I say.*

Take on an impossible battle.
Brag a little.
Create a rhyme about yourself.
Take back your name.
Give away your titles for something larger.

*I am the greatest, I said that even before I knew I was.*

# 34: CREATE SOME BUZZ

*F*lora, the goddess of flowers, married to the West Wind and mother to the God of Fruit—it is in her ear that this hive buzzes. [A paper wasp nest, to be exact, but its buzz led me to think of the buzz of bees.]

Her lips, according to Ovid, breathe spring roses. Her realm is not forests but gardens and fields, which no savage beast may enter.[96]

As Chase Purdy notes in an article from June 2019,

The US Department of Agriculture has said that one-in-three bites of food Americans take in can be tied back to the labor of bees, which buzz from plant to plant taking and delivering pollen. In all, bees pollinate about $15 billion worth of food crops in the US each year. On a global scale, it's estimated that somewhere between $235 billion and $577 billion worth of annual food production relies directly on bees. In all, about 84% of commercially grown crops are insect pollinated.[97]

The buzz: the bees are disappearing.

According to Karen Rennich of *Bee Informed*, "A persistent worry among beekeepers nationwide is that there are fewer and fewer favorable places for bees to land."[98]

Where have all the untainted flowers gone?
When will we ever learn?
When will we ever learn?

We have unloosed savage beasts into the garden: weed-killers, pesticides, neonicotinoids, "a witch's brew of pesticides and fungicides contaminating pollen that bees collect to feed their hives."[99]

What pleas do the bees buzz in Flora's ear?

It is the wind perhaps that carries our chemicals from crops to weeds to gardens to wildflowers. A beast has entered Flora's sacred realm, after an eternity of her watchfulness and protection.

Flora, can you get your husband the West-Wind to stop blowing?

How many bees must disappear from Earth before we perceive the sting?

Maybe the bees whisper of crocuses, sweet alyssum, heliotrope, scarlet sage, torenia, the rose mallow, shirley poppy, nigella, love in a mist, monkshood, wolf's bane, anemônê, khrysokomê, larkspur, daphnê, linden, lotus, moly, myrtle, narcissus, sweet violet, the red, red rose dyed by the blood of Aphrodite's dying dearest Adonis.[100]

Faced with what might seem to be endless loss and destruction, this new age counters with buzz: a throng of tweets, a brood of blogs, a mass of messages, a pack of posts, a bevy of viral videos, a nest of shots, a flight of flash fiction, a press of poems, a school of songs.

Even the word itself buzzes.

The earth is melting.
The bees are disappearing.
The children are being caged.
The schoolkids are practicing getting shot.
We've filled our jails with people of color.
#metoo.

Buzz.

Save the bees.
Save the earth.
Save our souls.
Save our kids.
Save our brothers and sisters.

Buzz. Buzz. Bu—

# 35: FLY YOURSELF TO THE MOON

*I*n our dreams, we can fly. "In almost every culture," Jeffrey Sumber writes, "flying dreams represent freedom or a release from daily pressures."[101]

In flight, we are free.

In this photo, the sun appears to me in the background, evoking Icarus, Daedalus' son, who flew too close to his own sun, thus melting the wax fastening his wings, thus falling into the sea and drowning.

His father Daedalus also was the builder of the Labyrinth for the Minotaur.

An amaze-ing inventor, that Daedalus.

The consequences of taking flight is burning up, falling back to the Earth.

In my own flight dreams, I often wave to those still grounded. Hello? Goodbye? The skies are always empty; the ground, full. No sun, no moon, no stars, no clouds.

Our dreams always place the waking ego in a symbolic landscape that reflects the collective, conventional attitudes and opinions of our given society or culture, while at the same time pointing to the larger, more universal human needs that may or may not be met by that particular society. Thus, dreams always tend to subvert prematurely closed attitudes and ideologies. Even if a religious intuition was first born from the same collective unconscious source as our dreams, as soon as authentic spiritual inspiration becomes frozen in creed and dogma, the dreams themselves will begin to criticize and subvert it in the interest of the next evolution of psychospiritual wholeness that the dogmatic formulation closes off prematurely.[102]

Against dogma, we take flight. In this age of increasingly closed-off ideas and attitudes, the dream-sky must be filled to the brim with fliers.

Boy, are my arms tired.

On earth, the Labyrinth twists and turns, trapping, confusing, hiding a Monster; in the sky, no walls, no paths, just the light of the sun, drawing us in.

In this photo, the flower chooses flight, to leave behind roots and earth for something more universal.

What need, oh flower!, is not being met at this particular time in this particular garden? What binds you, confines you, holds you down?

I wandered lonely as a cloud
That floats on high o'er vales and hills,
When all at once I saw a crowd,
A host, of golden daffodils;
Beside the lake, beneath the trees,
Fluttering and dancing in the breeze.

Continuous as the stars that shine
And twinkle on the milky way,
They stretched in never-ending line
Along the margin of a bay:
Ten thousand saw I at a glance,
Tossing their heads in sprightly dance.[103]

This week, look at your own flights of fancy, at the landscape for what it might symbolize, to see what universal needs it might be pointing you towards.

Your own self might be an archetype, your own flight a journey to find the boon that will save our wasted world from itself.

Take-off.

And nail that landing.

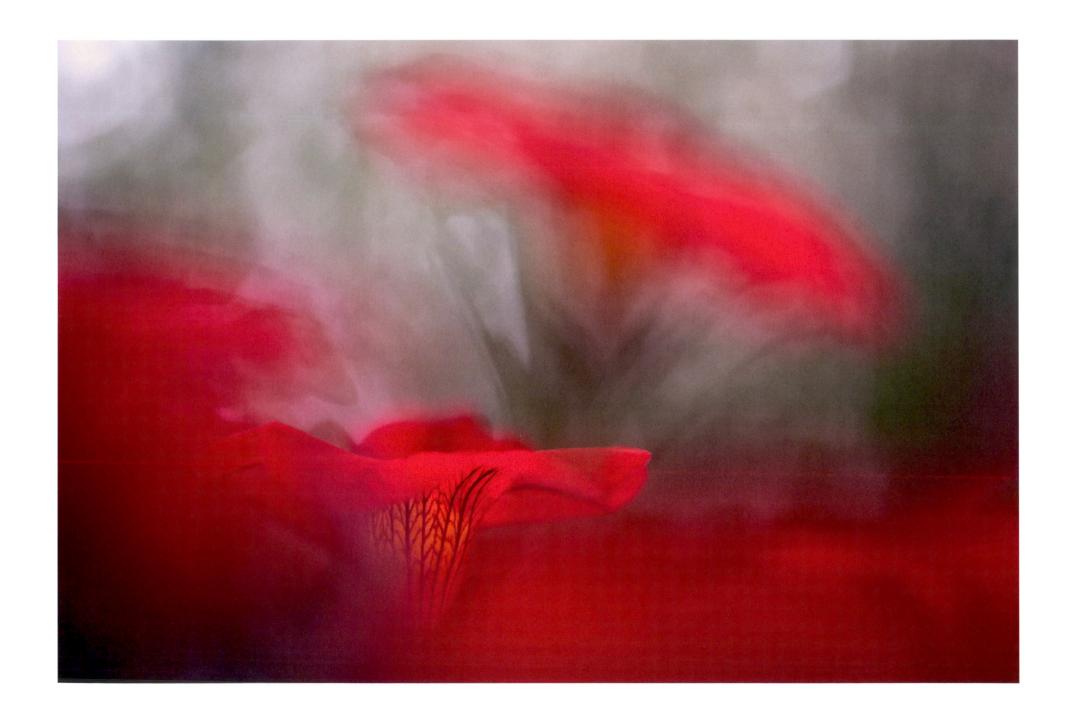

# 36: ORDER YOURSELF ORIFLAMME

**Chiefly poetic.** Something resembling the oriflamme of St Denis in colour; (hence) a bright, conspicuous object.[104]

Throughout history and across cultures, the color red has held strong symbolic meaning. Red is the color of romance—think red roses. Red is also associated with sexuality—think the Lady in Red. Red is also linked to physical aggression—think blood. But the scarlet hue may also wield a kind of psychological power—one that appears to be out of our conscious awareness.[105]

Dominance, sexual attractiveness, achievement—all these things might be affected by our heightened awareness of redness; "for example, a series of four experiments found that the fleeting sight of red before an IQ test or important exam was found to impair performance."[106]

However, according to Snopes, the claim that "red cars are ticketed for speeding more often than vehicles of other colors" is false.

*What's black and white and red all over?*

"That joke appeared in at least 21 collections of folk riddles published between 1917 and 1974."[107]

So the answer to the riddle—*what's read all over?*—is perhaps the riddle itself.

To be red is to be conspicuous, not so much so that you get more speeding tickets than your share, but enough to distract your viewers, make them stupid, excited, or perceiving threats wherever red pops up.

In M. Night Shyamalan's *The Sixth Sense*, "the color red is intentionally absent from most of the film, but it is used prominently in a few isolated shots for 'anything in the real world that has been tainted by the other world' and 'to connote really explosively emotional moments and situations.'"[108]

I see red, people.

Red lives at the end of the visible light spectrum; "light just past this range is called infrared, or below red, and cannot be seen by human eyes, although it can be sensed as heat." Also, "at sunrise and sunset, when the path of the sunlight through the atmosphere to the eye is longest, the blue and green components are removed almost completely, leaving the longer wavelength orange and red light."[109]

Maybe the answer to the riddle of red's power over us exists in the color itself.

It exists on the boundary between seeing and sensing, visible and invisible, day and night, waking and dreaming.

While red enhances our sexual attraction, it also impairs our performance, its link to dominance and aggression a reminder to us of the stakes involved in our actions.

Oedipus famously came across riddles. The Sphinx posed, "What is the creature that walks on four legs in the morning, two legs at noon and three in the evening?" And later, Thebes asks him "Who killed King Laius?"

For both riddles, Oedipus himself was the answer.

He who read riddles better than anyone alive didn't see that one coming.

Maybe, red asks us, to consider that the question(s) of the world cannot be answered with rationality; maybe the invisible world just below red makes the world go round.

This week, order yourself an oriflamme. Go get your red on.

# 37: TAKE A STAND FOR HUMANITY

*I*s there one book or song or poem or movie or piece of art you return to again and again?

For me, it's Sophocles' *Antigone*, the story of the princess of Thebes. Her brother's corpse—as punishment for attacking his own city—was to be left unburied, rotting at the city gates, his flesh to be picked at by the birds. The first law of the new King, Antigone's uncle, is to forbid burying him. The penalty for doing so: death.

*There's something we must do*, Antigone tells her sister. *Bury the brother.*

But you'll die.

*I'm no traitor. Not to the gods. Not to my brother.*

It's the family's duty to bury a loved one, a religious obligation to the gods and goddesses.

It's ours, the State tells her.

She doesn't stand for it.

The Self versus the State. That body at the city's gates—to whom does it belong? Who has power over it?

Antigone buries the body, receives the State's punishment, an ironic one. It is she who will be buried.

Alive.

When I first saw this image of that focused-flower against the blur of the others, I thought of Antigone, the lone figure in Thebes to take a stand against the State that claimed ownership of a body it had no right to.

Antigone's plight, according to Bonnie Honig, helps tragedicians "explore the possibilities of action in conditions of seeming impossibility."[110] But Honig sees something else:

Antigone who not only resists but also quests for sovereignty, who is oriented to life not primarily to death, who acts on behalf of both singularity and equality, sometimes in concert with others, plotting, conspiring, and navigating her way through *logos* (reason) and *phonê* (voice), mimicry, parody, and double entendre, which also work their way through her.[111] Sophocles' Antigone can be seen to ask: how should the *polis* (community) treat others (from traitor to *polis* hero, from dissident resister to mourning mother) in life and in death?[112]

So many of us have taken inspiration from Antigone's stand, and the meaning of that stand is as varied as the people who've been inspired by her. For me, she stands for the desire to be heard, to be seen, to be considered, to matter in a world that seeks to silence, erase. She stands against Power, wanting it for herself.

What is the commonality that connects us all? The thing we might all stand for? Is it our shared boundaries, our shared limited time on Earth, our desire to be heard, to be seen, to be counted and considered?

Consider Antigone, the Greek princess who took a stand, who said her body didn't belong to the State.

It belonged to her.

And her alone.

This week, consider that isolated stand against the blurred masses, both the courage of such a stand and the awful consequences.

It asks you to stand with the resister.

It asks you to take such a stand yourself.

It asks you to consider both the Power of a stand and the Powers that might arise to topple those who stand against.

Consider this: what you might stand against.

Consider, too, whom or what you might stand for.

# 38: TAKE TIME FOR A SHELTER

eg, our invisible photographer, calls this image "Shelter," a word that perhaps has its origins in *shield*.

Safety. It's a basic human need that, once met, allows us to get on with more important things, like contemplating our own deaths:

Once a person has met his deficiency needs, the focus of his anxiety shifts to self-actualization and he begins—even if only at a subconscious or semiconscious level—to contemplate the context and meaning of life. He may come to fear that death is inevitable and that life is meaningless, but at the same time cling on to the cherished belief that his life is eternal or at least important. This gives rise to an inner conflict that is sometimes referred to as 'existential anxiety' or, more colourfully, as 'the trauma of non-being'.... Facing up to non-being enables a person to put his life into perspective, see it in its entirety, and thereby give it a sense of direction and unity. If the ultimate source of anxiety is a fear of the future, the future ends in death; and if the ultimate source of anxiety is uncertainty, death is the only certainty. Facing up to death, accepting its

inevitability, and integrating it into life not only cures one of neurosis, but also enables one to get and make the most out of life. [113]

Perhaps this image captures an internal conflict we all face between shielding ourselves from death and accepting its inevitability. The shield allows us to be, gives us the safety needed to contemplate our non-being.

*If I were asked to name the chief benefit of the house, I should say: the house shelters day-dreaming, the house protects the dreamer, the house allows one to dream in peace.*
—Gaston Bachelard

Prometheus stole fire for humanity to make us superior to nature, giving us the ability to create such a shelter, a shelter that separated us from our natural selves, a separation that led to Nature's having a power over us. Without shelter, we are overpowered by Nature; with it, we lose our connection to Nature, our understanding of it, our power over it.

There's no winning, is there?

Sheltered, we can at least dream in peace. We can shield ourselves, and thus not only accept our deaths, but create the space for our afterlives.

The theory of a natural afterlife defines a vastly different, real possibility. The natural afterlife embodies all of the sensory perceptions, thoughts, and emotions present in the final moment of a near-death, dreamlike experience. With death this moment becomes timeless and everlasting to the dying person—essentially, a never-ending experience.[114]

In our shelters, we learn to accept our finitude; they give us the space we need for our final endless dream.

This week's image invites you to focus on your shelter.

Create within it a space, no matter how tiny, for day-dreaming. Add objects to that space that speak to you of shelter, of a private self that is yours and yours alone.

Now, close your eyes.

And dream a little.

# 39: SEIZE THE SURREAL DAY

ow many surrealists does it take to screw in a light bulb?

A fish.

I remember mistaking an old woman for a trout stream in Vermont, and I had to beg her pardon.

"Excuse me," I said. "I thought you were a trout stream."

"I'm not," she said.[115]

In the early 20th century, several avant-garde movements, including the dadaists, surrealists, and futurists began to argue for an art that was random, jarring and illogical. The goals of these movements were in some sense serious, and they were committed to undermining the solemnity and self-satisfaction of the contemporary artistic establishment. As a result, much of their art was intentionally amusing.[116]

I came across two flowers. They were practicing their dance routine.

"It looks like a ballet," I said.

The one closest to me answered, "We've rejected classical ballet." The flower curled her petals up, then down. "This is a contemporary dance."

"What do you call it?" I asked.

"Swan Lake."

"But that's the world's greatest ballet!"

She performed a single chasse. "Not the way we do it."

I wonder where that fish has gone.
You did love it so. You looked after it like a son.
And it went wherever I did go.

Is it in the cupboard?
Yes! Yes! No!…

Wouldn't you like to know?
It was a lovely little fish.
And it went wherever I did go.
It's behind the sofa!
Where can that fish be?
It is a most elusive fish!
And it went wherever I did go.

Ooooh, fishy, fishy, fishy fish!
A-fish, a-fish, a-fish, a-fishy, ooooh.
Ooooh, fishy, fishy, fishy fish!
That went wherever I did go.[117]

Two flowers walk into a bar. Without looking up, the barkeep asks, "Would you like a beer"—and looks up, sees the flowers—"Orchids."

"Just the beer," they both answer.

Two fish are in their tank.

"Why did the chicken cross the road?" asks one.

"What's a road?" replies the other. "And how do you drive this thing?

This week, take a walk on the surreal side.

Begin with your breakfast, your morning surreal, perhaps.

Put logic aside.

Be random.

Be jarring.

Be like two flowers practicing their contemporary dance interpretation of the classic ballet *Swan Lake*.

And if, along the way, you find that lost fish, please return it to its tank.

I think you'll find it in your local military museum.

# 40: TAKE A TRIP TO BOKEH

h, to be that bee in the photo, living it up in Bokeh, the foreground flowers on an entirely different plane, another dimension, so focused, attentive, like the kids who willingly sat in the front row.

In the back rows, all kind of things are going down: secret meetings, drug deals, an exchange of papers, a cornucopia of shenanigans.

In Bokeh, out of the spotlight, people can be themselves, can take off the masks, beclouded, be buzzed.

Bokeh, the blind obscure, transforms bodies into soap-bubbles. They float in the fog, forever un-popped.

In Bokeh, the visitors lose their focus, drop their guidebooks, cannot find their keys or wallets, find themselves blurring into the sweet, silky retreat from corporeality.

In Bokeh, while the kids in the front row raise their petals, the kids in the back write notes, slip them through the blur, watch them float as bubbles into the soft soap.

It's never scary in Bokeh. It's never too much. It's never a peppering of questions, a test you never knew about it and never studied for. There are no bells in Bokeh. No alarms. No active shooter, lock-down drills.

In that dim dazzle, you might find yourself losing your definitions; you might find your borders be-dimmed and be-damned; you might find yourself becoming one with everything.

Those flowers in the foreground! How they strain for attention, no amount enough to satisfy, to fill their lack, the holes in self.

Who drilled those holes? Who inserted that emptiness?

Can we blame Adam & Eve? Is that lack we feel the distance between us and the heavens, between Eden & Earth?

Did it all take place in the nursery? With what our caregivers gave and withheld?

Or is it that we are born into a language that creates distance between us and the world?

Is it that society creates pre-designed roles for ourselves to fit into?

Does consumerism fill us with holes so we'll fill them with products to complete us?

In the Bokeh, no one reaches for things to fill themselves with. In the Bokeh, they don't make fun of the hands in the front reaching for answers. They don't pay them any attention. In the Bokeh, the bee disappears without so much as a single buzz.

They are singing: "At the Bokeh, Bokeh-cabana… The Bokeh invites lack.

At the Bokeh, no one keys in, knuckles down, just does it.

No one falls for anyone or anything.

At the Bokeh.

Nowhere is passion and nothing is fashion.

At the Bokeh.

This week, take a brief vacay in the soupy soap of Bokeh's blur.

*How do I get there?*, you ask.

Write your way there.

# 41: GO GLOBAL, BABY

*I*f you are of a certain age of which I am, you might remember globes, world globes, spinning them around and around, then placing your finger on the twirling world.

Did the world seem so small or so big?

You might also remember the World Book Encyclopedias, bought from a young traveling salesperson, door-to-door, invited in because your mother felt bad for him.

Years later, she won't feel bad enough for you to buy a set of Cutco knives.

In 2007, Thomas Friedman revisited his notion that *The World is Flat*:

Of course the world is not flat. But it isn't round anymore, either. I have found that using the simple notion of flatness to describe how more people can plug, play, compete, connect, and collaborate with more equal power than ever before—which is what is happening in the world—really helps people who are trying to understand the essential impact of all the technological changes coming together today. [118]

In the 21st century, the world is flat. Again.

In the Internet era, the availability of communications technology and social media like YouTube, Facebook and Twitter have made it easy for individuals, famous or not, to spread disinformation and attract others to their erroneous ideas. One of the topics that has flourished in this environment is that of the flat Earth. [119]

Technology—more specifically social media—has flattened the earth, transformed globes into antiques. Flatness is not without its consequences. With a flat earth, according to the Earth Institute at Columbia University, we'd face the following:

(1) A pancaked earth might not have any gravity;

(2) It's unclear what force would keep the sun and moon hovering above the Earth… instead of crashing into it.

(3) There'd also have to be an explanation for what happens to plates at the edge of the world. One could imagine they might fall off, but that would presumably jeopardize the proposed [ice] wall that prevents people from falling off the disk-shaped world. [120]

A flat world, so it seems, continually tries to toss people off its edges while, from above, the Moon and Sun engage in a game of celestial dodgeball, with the two of them the only ones holding the balls.

That same article remind us that "the idea that many people—including the Spaniards and Christopher Columbus—believed the Earth to be flat was largely concocted by 19th century writers such as Washington Irving, Jean Letronne and others."

Since 3rd century B.C. and beyond, the world wasn't flat for most folks. But the flat earth returns to us, flattened by the technological marvels that threaten to throw us all off into the ether.

Or instead of being pummeled by the heavens, we might instead be hit by the disapproval of the Social Media Influencers, whoever they might be at any given time.

This global image reminds you to turn off, tune out, and drop in to the world. Check out the encyclopedias in a library, spin a record, touch your finger to a globe.

Did you know vinyl in 2019 outsold CDs for the first time since 1986?

Write in a notebook.

Mail a letter.

Turn off.

Tune out.

Drop in.

# 42: SET A PART-TIME TRAP

*Cosmos: The Science of Everything* explains the relationship of ants and pitcher plants:

Ants are drawn to pitcher plants by the deliciously sweet nectar oozing from the inner margin of a mature pitcher's rim. An ant unlucky enough to be walking across a wet peristome will slip and fall into the waiting pool of digestive juices at the bottom of the trap.[121]

So, you would think, keeping the trap oozing full-time would be the best way to trap ant after ant after ant. Not so.

Instead of keeping their peristomes moist with extra nectar when there's no rainfall or dew, one species of pitcher plants was found to allow them to dry out for up to eight hours a day.[122]

Was that smart? A study decided to compare the performance of part-time and full-time traps. To do so, they did the following:

They compared the amount of prey caught by pitchers on a drip to natural, 'untreated' pitchers. To their surprise, the natural pitchers captured twice as many ants. While the trapped prey wasn't evenly distributed —some pitchers captured huge numbers of ants and others captured none—only the naturally wet/dry plants managed to capture ants in batches.[123]

The scout ant that finds the nectar and dry peristome brings back a batch of friends to bring home the booty. This booty call sometimes benefits the ants and sometimes benefits the pitcher plant, who might get lucky with some rain just as the ant colony descends upon the nectar at the rim.

We have much to learn from this week's image, of ants marching along a pitcher plant's edge.

Ask yourself: *Is the peristome wet or dry?* And you'll see how everything changes.

In dreams, the symbolism of the trap has everything to do with if you're setting one or stuck in one, whether it's bird trap or bear trap, a trap door or a booby trap. In any case, it seems better to be the trapper rather than the trapped.

In short, a trap means "a readiness to take action...to break out of a rut...to explore opportunities."[124] It isn't easy to capture what we want; sometimes, to do so, we need to set a trap.

The problem with traps are many, but one major one, of course, is that something unintended might get caught.

Image a pitcher plant catching Bigfoot! Clearly, that would be a problem.

The perfect trap, it seems, might be one that is part-time, mutually beneficial, and only catches what is intended.

So, that is the mission for this week, oh my. Create the perfect trap.

Here are the top ten keys to the perfect trap:

1. Keep your peristome intermittently wet and dry.

2. Create signs, such as: "No Bigfoots allowed."

3. Ooze a delicious treat on the inner margins.

4. Fill the bottom of the trap with newspaper, preferably the funny pages.

5. Entice scouts with your friendly welcome.

6. Hope the scouts' friends don't have a party that night.

7. Text scout a picture of the nectar-filled rim.

8. Sweeten nectar with pure cane sugar.

9. Ooze more.

10. Pray for rain.

That's it.
Now go set those traps.

# 43: LIVE IN YOUR OWN WORLD

 *live in my own little world. But it's ok, they know me here.* —Lauren Myracle[125]

Home. A person's house or abode, the place where a person lives or was raised, native country, homeland. Does it call us with its siren song or warn us away like the sirens of an alarm?

*For the two of us, home isn't a place. It is a person.* —Stephanie Perkins[126]

Dogs know such a truth about homes, don't they? Home alone, for them, isn't home at all. Can that person Perkins references above be your self? Surely.

But not if you're a dog.

There is something transcendent about little worlds, with their itsy-bitsy canvasses and their teensy-weensy moments of colossal significance. That is the fun of tiny worlds, yes? To make them all that there is, to blow them up and up and up until they are everything.

I imagine these two figures in the photo have created such a world, a tiny world made by them that has become everything. I imagine an apocalyptic event, so they are all that is left, they and their tiny house. They and that pink backpack and brown hat.

I imagine they miss Her immensely. They have gripped each other's hand so tightly that the two hands have become one.

They see Her everywhere in that house.
But they can't leave it.
There's nowhere else they'd rather be.

*We leave something of ourselves behind when we leave a place, we stay there, even though we go away. And there are things in us that we can find again only by going back there.*
—Pascal Mercier[127]

We are all ghosts, our homes stuffed with our presence.

*Home is where one starts from.* —T.S. Eliot

Our own homes begin with Prometheus, and the crime for which he is punished by Zeus: everyday while he was chained to a rock, an eagle ate Prometheus' liver.

In some traditions, Prometheus made the first man from clay, whilst in others, the gods made all creatures on Earth, and Epimetheus and Prometheus were given the task of endowing them with gifts so that they might survive and prosper. Epimetheus liberally spread around such gifts as fur and wings but by the time he got around to [humans], he had run out of gifts. Feeling sorry for [our] weak and naked state, Prometheus raided the workshop of Hephaistos and Athena on Mt. Olympus and stole fire, and by hiding it in a hollow fennel-stalk, he gave the valuable gift to [humans] which would help [them] in life's struggle. The Titan also taught [us] how to use [the] gift and so the skill of metalwork began; he also came to be associated with science and culture.[128]

Home arrives to help us in life's struggle. Did Prometheus know that home would also be our life's struggle? Did Prometheus know some of us would create our own little worlds, built not out of fire and metal and wood and nails but out of the ethereal, out of light, out of time.

This week, create a little world, live in it for a bit until it feels like home.

# 44: GET IN ON THE SECRET

**insider**
One who is inside; a person who is within the limits of some place, society, organization, etc.; hence, one in possession of special information, one who is 'in the secret'. Opposed to *outsider*.[129]

According to a 2017 article, Finland Is Still the World's Best Kept Secret. You would not know this secret, even if you went to Finnishing school. There are other secrets, none of which of course any of us knows the answer to. They include these:

- The Hapsburg napkin folding technique.[130]
- KFC chicken recipe.[131]
- Chartreuse liquor *(There are only two monks in the entire world who know the secret recipe).*[132]
- Synchronized fireflies — what is it?[133]
- What's the fate of the Ark of the Covenant?[134]
- The Moai statues of Easter Island: How did they get there?[135]
- The best place to eat in [City name].
- The best secret resort in [Country].
- Where is Jimmy Hoffa?
- Where did I put my keys?

Insiders know the answers to all these mysteries and more. They know how to get tickets to sold-out events, how to get into private clubs, where to get the best wines, the best barbecue wings, the best seats for the best events in all the best cities.

But there are other kinds of insiders, like our invisible photographer, who throughout this book reveals to us this insider's look at the natural world.

This kind of insider has supernatural vision, not x-ray, not the kind that burns through vaults, but the kind that envisions the world magically, particularly, beautifully. Want to develop your own insider's vision? Here are some tips from *ALLWOMENSTALK:*

1. Look around you.
2. Keep a scrapbook.
3. Don't be afraid.
   …
5. Identify what intrigues you.
6. Use your camera.
7. Books.[136]

What of that missing #4? Its suggestion—*create, don't imitate*—didn't seem in tune with the heart of this book. As Katey Schultz, one of my writing coaches, reminds us, "Imitation is iteration, and iteration leads to innovation and creativity."

That's what insiders provide: the advice behind the advice, the real scoop, the bend in the rules, the openness to go where others have gone in that desire to find innovation, creativity, one's own "inside" self.

This kind of insider creates new worlds out of a flock of fennel, out of a puff of phlox, the peristome of pitcher plants, the bokeh blur, fern shadows, the inside of a lily.

The more obscure meanings of *insider* refer to the inside vest pocket or someone riding on the inside of a vehicle, as opposed, I imagine, to the persons riding on the roof.

An out-rider.

This week, look around, put your fears aside, find what intrigues you, put your nose inside some books—and then grab your camera and create!

And, if along the way, you find my keys or Jimmy Hoffa, please let someone know.

# 45: ACT FUNNY AND DON'T KNOW Y

urple Haze.
What is it?
A dream of Prince.

Purple is associated with spirituality, the sacred, higher self, passion, third eye, fulfillment, and vitality. Purple helps align oneself with the whole of the universe… Because the purple color is created by combining a strong warm with a strong cool color, the color retains both warm and cool properties. On one hand, the color purple can boost imagination and creativity; on the other, too much purple can cause moodiness.[137]

In 1985, Rolling Stone asked Prince: 'What do you think about the comparisons between you and Jimi Hendrix?' His reply: 'It's only because he's black. That's really the only thing we have in common. He plays different guitar than I do. If they really listened to my stuff, they'd hear more of a Santana influence than Jimi Hendrix. Hendrix played more blues; Santana played prettier. You can't compare people, you really can't, unless someone is blatantly trying to rip somebody off. And you can't really tell that unless you play the songs.' Later that year, he told MTV, 'Hendrix is very good. Fact. There will never be another one like him, and it would be a pity to try. I strive for originality in my work, and hopefully, it'll be perceived that way.'[138]

Was Prince the heir to Jimi Hendrix? He was known to bristle at the analogy, but then—in keeping with his famously quirky persona—ended up re-doing (and renaming) 'Red House' from 1967's *Are You Experienced* anyway. He also sampled the fan favorite 'Machine Gun,' and was even reportedly considering an all-Hendrix tribute show in the months before his April 2016 death. Prince quickly shot that idea down, but it would have made perfect sense to all of the armchair musicologists who so consistently tried to connect the two.[139]

Influences. We bristle at comparisons, at the notion that some other artist gave birth to us, that we didn't arrive on the scene like Athena, fully-formed.
A mash-up of "Purple Rain" & "Purple Haze" might go like this:

Yeah, purple rain all in my eyes
Don't know what I'm singing up here
C'mon, raise your mind
Purple haze or just the end of time
Only want to see you
In the purple haze,
Purple haze, purple haze…

Asked if he needed anything before taking the stage at the Super Bowl, Prince famously quipped, "Can you make it rain harder?"

This week, embrace, renounce, or embr-ounce your influences.
Whether you want to party like it's 1999 or bust down the door of that red house yonder, this week you need to find an "act" that came before you, and in some way play tribute to that act.

And if you ever find it raining during your super moment, channel a little Prince.

"Can you make it rain harder?"

# 46: GIVE A THING ITS OTHER NAME

Juliet:

'Tis but thy name that is my enemy;
Thou art thyself, though not a Montague.
What's Montague? It is nor hand, nor foot
Nor arm, nor face, nor any other part
Belonging to a man. O, be some other name!
What's in a name? That which we call a rose
By any other name would smell as sweet.

Rose, of the genus Rosa, in the family Rosaceae.

A kenning is a type of circumlocution, in the form of a compound that employs figurative language in place of a more concrete single-word noun. Kennings are strongly associated with Old Norse and later Icelandic and Old English poetry. They usually consist of two words, and are often hyphenated. For example, Old Norse poets might replace 'sword' with an abstract compound such as 'wound-hoe.'[140]

A bee might instead be called *a flower-farmer*; the clouds, *sky-curtains*; butterflies, *silk-kites*; the day, *candle-snuffer*; the dusk, *shadow-meld*.

Juliet's innocence—that there is nothing in a name—allows that love to burn as brightly as it does; but it's that same innocence that destroys that love, making it blind to the world's walls, the world's boundaries, its poisons, its names.

What's in a name? she asks. "A person's name," answers Dale Carnegie, "is to him or her the sweetest and most important sound in any language." And as *The Washington Post* argues, "A person's name is the greatest connection to their own identity and individuality. Some might say it is the most important word in the world to that person."[141]

Would a Romeo by any other name still be a Romeo? Or might he be Flash-Feeling, Innocence-Intelligence, or Juliet-Addict?

Does this other name change identity, individuality?

Aren't names just random words we've attached to things that have little or nothing do with the Real?

Juliet dreams of a world where names can be erased, so that erasing the Montague from Romeo's name erases the history of that ancient feud, the origins of which no one can remember anyway. Let the great re-naming commence! In renaming, Juliet claims the world for her own vision, where roses, even though they might be called Thorn-Flushes, still smell as sweet.

"The mere fact of naming an object," writes George Eliot, "tends to give definiteness to our conception of it—we have then a sign which at once calls up in our minds the distinctive qualities which mark out for us that particular object from all others."[142]

All opinion, Eliot argues, all science is naming.

To name is to change, to redefine. People fight over what to be referred to in the language, what pronoun refers back to them, because they understand that names define, that if the name doesn't exist in the language, then it doesn't exist at all.

They fight for the right to name.

This week, give things their rightful names, the distinctive name, the particular name. Don't be afraid to summon a kenning to cast your naming spell.

Understand the power you are calling upon.

The power to name.

ABOVE  104

# 47: DELIVER SOME PUN-ISHMENT

When I saw this photograph of a White Swan Coneflower looking down upon another White Swan Coneflower, I immediately thought of this sentimental quote: *I'm sure wherever my dad is he's looking down on us… he's not dead… just very condescending.*[143]

The one-liner might be the "joke" equivalent of the micro fiction or the macro photo. Pith and power pack its punch. It redirects your attention quickly and sharply. It makes the very small very significant.

*When I was a boy, I would lay in my twin sized bed and wonder where my brother was.* —Mitch Hedberg

Sarah Silverman (book titles): *The Bedwetter: Stories of Courage, Redemption, and Pee.*

*So I'm at the wailing wall, standing there like a moron, with my harpoon.* —Emo Philips

*I'd kill for a Nobel Peace Prize.* —Steven Wright

During my teens, while my friends were being punished for underage drinking or staying out past curfew, I was kicked out of the house by my father for punning. No joke.

I told him, on my way out, that I'd go to the pharmacy for some pun-icillion.

*I'd like to think that halfway through Nicole Kidman's last name there's a tiny bar mitzvah.* —Megan Amran

*How to make a million dollars: First, get a million dollars.* —Steve Martin

*The worst time to have a heart attack is during a game of charades.* —Demetri Martin

Humor is an excellent part of life. Laughing leads to increased pleasure, more enjoyment, and a happier life. At times, humor is certainly used to mask underlying 'truths' of the individual. In other instances, it is simply an outrageous thought leading to humor. Often, it is simply a reflection of our human desire to connect and experience joy. You do not have to give credence to every thought you have. One would benefit from evaluating his or her thinking and determining personal truth. Hopefully, that truth leads to joy, for both you and others.[144]

"I'm here today," says stand-up Wanda Sykes, "because I hated everything else." At the other end of the joke, we find the comedian, spilling out line after line, hoping one connects.

A punch line.

*When I said I was going to become a comedian, they all laughed. Well, they're not laughing now, are they?* —Bob Monkhouse

This week, deliver a knockout punch by throwing a one-liner at the appropriate time. Such a process, of course, means that you memorize a few, or write them down with your puncil.

Also, look for an opening to create your own. Do this enough times, and you'll become punstoppable.

*Two cannibals are eating a clown, and one looks at the other and says, Does this taste funny to you?*

# 48: DON'T BE KOI ABOUT YOUR GIFT

Hubris—an abundance of self-confidence—dooms humanity, time and time again, in story after story, ending after tragic ending.

A slice of humble pie a day keeps the doom away. We might begin to think of humility wrongly, "as low self-esteem or self-denigration," but *Psychology Today* defines it as such:

> The humble person keeps her accomplishments, gifts, and talents in a proper perspective. She has self-knowledge, and is aware of her limitations as an individual and as a human being. But humble individuals are also oriented towards others, they value the welfare of other people and have the ability to 'forget themselves' as well, when appropriate.[145]

*I have three precious things which I hold fast and prize. The first is gentleness; the second is frugality; the third is humility, which keeps me from putting myself before others. Be gentle and you can be bold; be frugal and you can be liberal; avoid putting yourself before others and you can become a leader.*
—Lao Tzu

To be hubristic is to lack humility, is to be oriented toward the Self without fully knowing it or its limitations. At the other extreme exists self-negation, self-harm:

> The self-directed violence is at first directed at the individual by and from hostile others who do not recognize or acknowledge the harm they cause, which has to be made manifest through other means, self-harm behavior being one of them. In this way, self-harm can be seen as a coping mechanism in that it is a silent protest—to manifest the harm that is so normative that it remains invisible to others, and thereby to manifest the social injury silently done.[146]

Here, in describing the self-harm behaviors of queer young adults, the author focuses our attentions on the origin of that harm, in the hostile gaze of the phobic-world.

It's no wonder that gifts get hidden away from the world's prying, hate-filled glare.

A silent protest.

A coping mechanism.

The hubris of that world! Such pain it inflicts upon our fellow humans!

What the world needs now is humility, he said with great confidence.

*To learn which questions are unanswerable, and not to answer them: this skill is most needful in times of stress and darkness.* —Ursula K. Le Guin, *The Left Hand of Darkness*

People gaze upon the world through a particular filter of ideas, skills, desires and expectations, framed by social class, gender, nationality, age and education. Gazing is a performance that orders, shapes and classifies, rather than reflects the world.[147]

This week's image understands that the world's gaze is often full of harm, a harm "so normative that it remains invisible to others." Against that harm that negates the self, the image asks you to assert the self, to find humility in that assertion. But the image also understands that it asks such an assertion perhaps from a position of privilege, as if such an act—the putting forth of self in a world hostile to it—doesn't have different consequences for each of our fellow humans.

So, with humility and hope, the image asks you for your presence, for your gifts.

# 49: BRING ON THE FIREWORKS

**S**omeone just lit a fireworks display against the backdrop of a purple pineapple!

None of that is literally true. Of course.

But it sure looks that way to me.

On a Friday night in the early 70s, you could easily find me in the wood-pannelled sunken family room with the brownie from my Salisbury steak TV dinner and the television parked on ABC: *The Brady Bunch, The Partridge Family, Room 222,* and *The Odd Couple.*

And, of course. *Love, American Style.* "Flutes, flutes, harp and flugelhorn set to a contemporary pop beat provided the 'love' ambiance."[148] The opening theme ended with fireworks and a superimposed graphic of a heart.

Boom, boom, boom!

And with that opening salvo, the 70s rush back: Marathon bars; red pistachio nuts; Saturday morning cartoons with Hong Kong Phooey, Josey and the Pussycats, Bugs and Scooby; a Slinky; the Sunday funnies on Silly Putty; Mary Poppins at the drive-in; London Broil; wheat germ; Quisp and King Vitamin cereals; Pop Rocks; Bubble-Yum; "I Will Survive." Soap.

How definitive those memories remain. How much they reveal about my own identity: race, class, geography, creed, and the like.

Ooh Ooh Mr. Kotter!

Who loves ya, baby.

What you see is what you get.

We are two wild and crazy guys!

Dy-No-Mite!

According to Richard Harris, a psychology professor at Kansas State University, using film quotes in everyday conversation is similar to telling a joke and a way to form solidarity with others.

People are doing it to feel good about themselves, to make others laugh, to make themselves laugh, Harris argues. He found that all of the participants in his study had used film quotes in conversation at one point or another. They overwhelmingly cited comedies, followed distantly by dramas and action adventure flicks.[149]

I say, "Marsha." You say, "Marsha." Together we say, "Marsha, Marsha, Marsha!"

And just like that we're bonded.

Launch the fireworks.

We're peeps.

Political correctness, the oppression of the left, a threat to free speech—all this appears more and more recently as enemies of the people, as something that forces people to shut up, silences them, indoctrinates them into identity politics. The world, a recent headline announces, is losing patience with the Wokesters.

But here's maybe something to consider, how every club created through culture excludes as much as it includes, that being reminded of how that exclusion might manifest itself into pain for others is maybe a very, very good thing to understand, to grasp. Maybe it's good no longer to be able to plead innocence, to blame those who are hurt with being too fragile, too sensitive, too "woke" for the broken world.

Now you know, the wokesters might be telling us, what you were once too blinded with the boom of fireworks to notice.

Maybe we look back to those times when anyone could say anything (the pain those words caused being silenced) with a weird nostalgia. Maybe we don't want to know.

What's bitten, though, cannot be unbitten.

What's been lit cannot be unlit.

This week, sure, look back, remember, but do so as woke as you want to be, aware that behind that amazing feeling of being included in a culture club lurks the equally strong feelings of those denied entrance.

# 50: WRITE YOUR FIFTY WORDS

Zoetrope Virtual Studio had a writing room called **The Flash Factory,** and each Sunday its host Richard Osgood would post five prompt words to be turned into a fifty-word piece of micro fiction. Here are some of those efforts, preceded by the five random words that prompted them.

*bubble sandwich etude cello salubrious*

### Usage
To my mom, they are bubble-head dolls. Squeeze sings "Pulling Muscles from Michelle." Golfers shoot out of bunkers using a "sand-wich," and Caesar said, "Etude, Brute." At rehab, I greet her with "Cello." She says, "It's so-lubrious here." Salubrious, I want to tell her, but resist. Nothing can stop her.

*arbor conspicuous banjo indigo destiny*

### On Arbor Day
Mom danced us among birches, the twigs hands, trunks swaying like middle school couples to Kiss's "Beth." I heard banjoes; my sister, Morrison. She'd learned colors from Crayola, called sky cerulean indigo. My mom named our dance Conspicuous Destiny. It meant we were doomed, like leaves, to twirl like crazy.

*dialect hopscotch partisan vernal monologue*

### If Only She'd Been Real
We used words no one else would, like "vernal precipitation" for April showers. We played hopscotch in dialect, what we imagined Hobbits sounded like. Before the next jump, we delivered a monologue that had to end with the word "partisan." She sparkled like fairy tales and wishes that went unanswered.

*omen whirligig adieu lark nor'easter*

### I've Still Got Something It Wants
The wind wants to topple; the rain to drown; the snow to bury; the twister to turn my home into a whirligig. The nor'easter awaits, a boogeyman. A lark, such thoughts, Harold says. A symptom of darker things. Each time, when Nature decides not to bid me adieu: an omen.

*shawl, mascot, barrel, lithograph, esplanade*

### Anniversary
They walked along the esplanade, a gull as mascot, almost perched upon her shawl. She pointed the barrel of her umbrella at a far-off ship. A passerby remarked, "It's like a lithograph." They fled the scene, panicked, as if pursued by the imaginary artist seeking to etch them into stone.

This week, try writing fifty words, using either the photograph as a prompt, five words gleaned from the image, or any random five words you come across.

Here's five to get you started, from the photo: *fire, bud, pedal, aperture, bokeh*. Fifty words. No more. No less.

# 51: TAKE 1 DOWN, PASS IT AROUND

*M*eg calls this one "Future Plans."
Below are 99 ideas for your own future.

1. Try not to blow it
2. Go to a museum
3. Send a postcard
4. Write a poem
5. Post a picture of your "space"
6. Watch an episode of *Scooby-Do*
7. Draw a monster. Why is it a monster?
8. Call an old friend
9. Write your own inspirational quote
10. Listen to an album you loved as a kid
11. Walk a dog for a canine rescue
12. Eat an atomic fireball
13. Take a stroll in a botanical garden
14. Watch a music video ("Once in a Lifetime")
15. Write down a dream
16. Create a diary entry for a fictional person
17. Tweet as an historical figure might have
18. Take a selfie with a stranger
19. Watch Spike Lee's *Do the Right Thing*
20. Snap some pictures in a photo booth
21. Watch Bugs in "What's Opera, Doc"
22. Play *Hamilton's* "My Shot" at volume 11
23. Learn a new subject
24. Surprise someone with a gift (this book?)
25. Wear bright colors
26. Binge *The Great British Baking Show*
27. Play Ella Fitzgerald's songbook albums
28. Embrace your shadow-self
29. Find funny flower names (*Hairy Woodrush*)
30. Rock polka-dots like Yayoi Kusama
31. Read Kathy Fish's *Wild Life Collected Works*
32. Follow Tony Gum on Instagram
33. Donate at https://alicenter.org/donate/
34. Finger paint
35. Shoot webs with Silly String
36. Did you Boscov today?
37. Bring out the board games (Rummikub?)
38. Read Tennessee Williams' "Oriflamme"
39. Stop and smell the flowers, literally
40. Sing aloud a hum of Pooh
41. Follow @megboscov on Instagram
42. Bake with fresh herb, uh, I mean herbs
43. Make yourself a Moscow Mule sans copper
44. Slow cook an African Peanut Stew
45. Read Toni Morrison's *Beloved*
46. Stay up late and sleep in the next day
47. *Shinrin-yoku:* forest bathing!
48. Bake cookies for a new neighbor
49. https://www.geocaching.com/play
50. Cook a new meal, recipe optional
51. Spend a night with your eyes on the skies
52. Watch the movie *Bringing Up Baby*
53. Plant your own succulent garden
54. Throw a non-Halloween costume party
55. Image search "Basquiat Paintings"
56. Send someone a care package
57. Learn how to make a vision board
58. Check out a local bookstore/camera shop
59. Read Fagles' translation of *Antigone*
60. Do something you've been putting off
61. Make (and eat) a favorite childhood meal
62. Take a class at a local arts center
63. Invite friends over for a movie marathon
64. Pop some popcorn (ok to use microwave)
65. Take a ghost tour of your favorite city
66. Enroll in Creative Live's curated classes
67. Watch anime *Death Note* on Netflix
68. Re-read a book from your childhood
69. Create a photo book for someone special
70. Volunteer at an assisted-living facility
71. Do a tiny thing to save the environment
72. Gather a few friends for a photo shoot
73. Build a fort, indoors or out
74. Give a toast when it's least expected
75. Pick a room and rearrange, a little or a lot
76. Make your own greeting card & send it
77. Watch or listen to Tig Notaro *Live*
78. Read flash fiction at smokelong.com
79. Subscribe to a print magazine or journal
80. Visit a show in a local art gallery
81. Send a stick to the ocean via the gutter
82. Collect loose change—and spend it all
83. Play Lucinda Williams' self-titled album
84. Take a bath with a bubble bath bomb
85. Memorize a (short) poem
86. Follow *Hand in Hand* playlist on Spotify
87. Make a cup of hot chocolate
88. Pick a new hairdo
89. Set a coins-snatched-off-elbow record
90. Watch S5 E1 of *The Dick Van Dyke Show*
91. Have a bonfire party: the smore the merrier
92. Watch Ali in *When We Were Kings*
93. Bring out an outfit you haven't yet worn
94. Ride a bike, unless you forget how to
95. Plan a picnic, indoors or out
96. Find a buddy for a weekly date (gym?)
97. Join a book or camera club
98. Eat some french fries
99. Just do…nothing

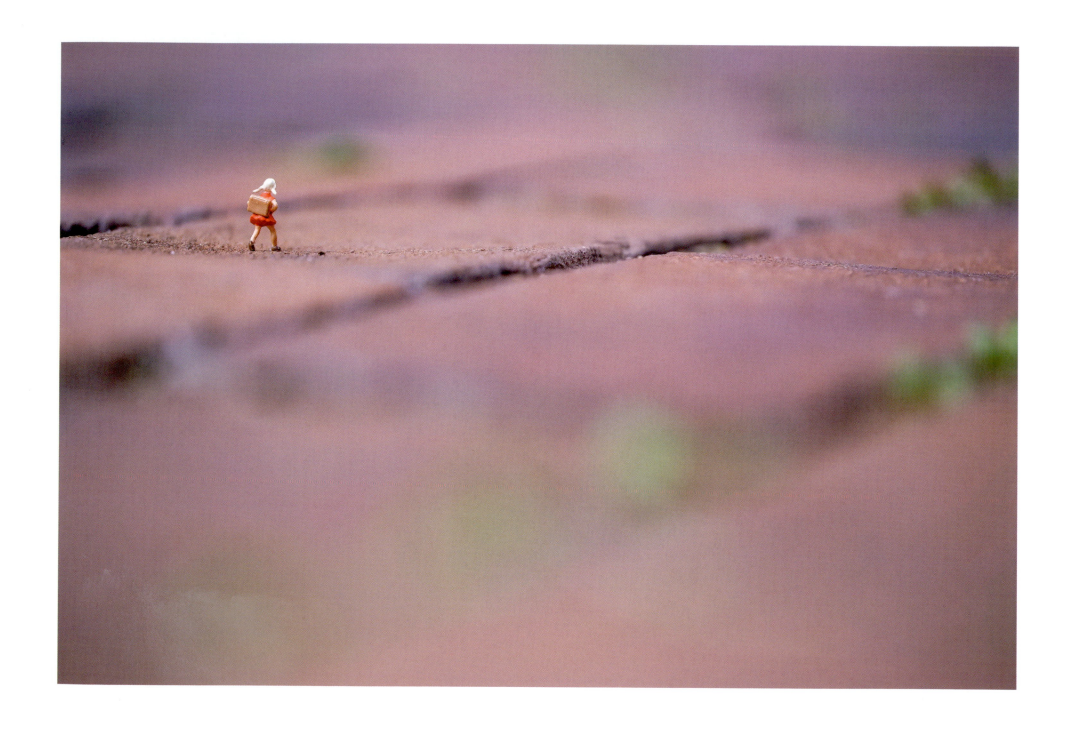

# 52: START SOMETHING NEW

*T*he end. In Baum's books, Dorothy returns to a Kansas that is missing its house, its broken beams scattered across Oz. It wasn't a dream. No way. She left.

Bonnie Friedman reminds us of the movie's changed ending in which Oz is a fantasy of Dorothy's subconscious:

> But Dorothy's not dreaming any more, she vows, 'I'm not going away ever, ever again.' 'Oh, Auntie Em,' she cries in her final declaration of love to the woman she quested for so well and long: 'There's no place like home.'

Friedman explains,

> Odysseus, is valued for his rich experience. Experience in a girl means just one thing, and it's no good. Leave home and you lose it, girls learn. Leave home, and home leaves you. The photo in your basket will transform. The woman who had smiled will die. The world is an alien, forsaken place; go into it and you will be alien and forsaken. Leave home, and you murder it. Only if you stay, can it, and you, be safe.[150]

But it was real! Stupid grown-ups. Stupid farm. Stupid Aunt. Stupid Uncle. At the end of the movie, Oz is taken away from Dorothy, from us all.

I once imagined a story in which Dorothy grew up to become Marion Crane in Psycho. Both as a young girl and as a grown woman she finds (spoiler alert!) a world of disguised men behind curtains, two curtains, each one pulled back, revealing a lie. The first uncovered the ugly truths of her world and then sent her back to live with them; and the second showed her that the promised escape offered by boys in parlors disguises yet another trap, cutting her out of the world, forever after.

At length, however, Dorothy sat up and looked about her.

'Good gracious!' she cried.

For she was sitting on the broad Kansas prairie, and just before her was the new farmhouse Uncle Henry built after the cyclone had carried away the old one.

Aunt Em had just come out of the house to water the cabbages when she looked up and saw Dorothy running toward her.

'My darling child!' she cried, folding the little girl in her arms and covering her face with kisses. 'Where in the world did you come from?'

'From the Land of Oz.'

Happily ever after. That's what we wish for at the end of this book.

Happily ever after.

May no one rip Oz from you.

Rip yourself from yourself.

At the end of this book, may you start your own journey.

Will you share it with us?—with the world? In spite of all the hostility that exists in the world?

How amazing, how courageous, how remarkable that, in spite of all those eyes behind curtains holding knives, you still venture out.

You still believe in Oz.

You still go. Both to home and away from it.

You start out, that tiny backpack pressed against your shoulders, the world infinitely large.

Happily ever after.

This book wishes you that and more.

With much love,

*Meg & Randy*

# Endnotes

1    "Signs and Symbols." *The Fitzwilliam Museum.* https://www.fitzmuseum.cam.ac.uk/pharos/collection_pages/northern_pages/PD_32_1968/TXT_BR_SS-PD_32_1968.htm.

2    Manusurov, Nasim. "What is a Mirrorless Camera." *Photography Life.* https://photographylife.com/what-is-a-mirrorless-camera.

3    King, Stephen. *On Writing: A Memoir of the Craft.* Kindle Edition. New York: Scribner, 2000. p. 105.

4    Berne, Eric. *The Happy Valley.* New York: Grove Press, 1968. Chapter 11.

5    Baum, L. Frank. *The Wonderful Wizard of Oz.* Chicago: Geo. M. Hill Co, 1900. p. 13.

6    Abbott, H. Porter. *The Cambridge Introduction to Narrative* (Cambridge Introductions to Literature). Cambridge University Press. Kindle Edition. p. 3.

7    Wolf, Marilyn. *Smart Camera Design: Algorithms, Architectures, and Art.* 1st Edition, Kindle Edition. Springer, 2017. Location 273.

8    "creature, n." *OED Online.* Oxford University Press, June 2019. https://www.oed.com/view/Entry/44082?redirectedFrom=creature#eid.

9    Berger, John. *Ways of Seeing.* New York: Penguin, 1990. p. 10.

10   Huxley, Francis. *The Way of the Sacred.* New York: Doubleday, 1974. p. 6.

11   Carroll, Henry. *Read This If You Want To Take Great Photographs.* London: Laurence King Publishing, 2004. p. 122.

12   Irvine, William B. *On Desire.* Oxford: Oxford University Press, 2006. p. 11.

13   Reiss, Steven Ph.D. *Who Am I?.* New York: Berkley Books, 2000. pp. 17-18.

14   Leader, Darian and Judy Groves. *Introducing Lacan.* New York: Totem Books, 1996. pp. 84-5.

15   Jung, Carl. *Modern Man in Search of a Soul.* New York: Routledge, 1933. p. 175.

16   Bakewell, Sarah. *At the Existentialist Café.* Kindle Edition. Great Britain: Chatto & Windus, 2016. p. 235.

17   Sexton, Anne. "Young." https://www.poemhunter.com/poem/young-14/. lines 18-23.

18   Jung, Carl. *Letters Volume I.* p. 33

19   Woolf, Virginia. *To the Lighthouse.* 1927. *Selected Works of Virginia Woolf.* Wordsworth Library Collection, 2007. p. 281.

20   Keller, Helen. "Helen Keller." *BrainyQuote.* https://www.brainyquote.com/quotes/helen_keller_132904.

21   Descartes, René. *Passions of the Soul.* 1649. https://www.earlymoderntexts.com/assets/pdfs/descartes1649part2.pdf.

22   Barth, Amy. "The Chemistry, Biology & Engineering That Make Spider Webs Awesome." *Discover: Science for the Curious.* September 2010. http://discovermagazine.com/2010/sep/06-chemistry-biology-engineering-awesome-spider-webs.

23   Harris, Tom. "How Spiders Work." *HowStuffWorks.com.* 8 August 2002. https://animals.howstuffworks.com/arachnids/spider.htm.

24   Picasso, Pablo. *BrainyQuote.* https://www.brainyquote.com/quotes/pablo_picasso_100864?src=t_spider.

25   Whitman, Walt. "A Noiseless Patient Spider." *Poetry Foundation.* https://www.poetryfoundation.org/poems/45473/a-noiseless-patient-spider.

26   Carroll, Henry. *Read This If You Want To Take Great Photographs.* London: Laurence King Publishing, 2004. p. 101.

27   Wilstach, Frank J., comp. "Soft." *A Dictionary of Similes.* Boston: Little, Brown, & Co., 1916. *Bartleby.com*, 2010. https://www.bartleby.com/161/2449.html.

28   "Soft Hearted Quotes." *Goodreads.* https://www.goodreads.com/quotes/tag/soft-hearted.

29   Wilstach, Frank J., comp. "Softly." *A Dictionary of Similes.* Boston: Little, Brown, & Co., 1916. *Bartleby.com*, 2010. https://www.bartleby.com/161/2450.html.

30   "William Butler Yeats." *BrainyQuote.* https://www.brainyquote.com/quotes/william_butler_yeats_146753?src=t_soft.

31   "Bokeh for Beginners." *Nikon.* https://www.nikonusa.com/en/learn-and-explore/a/tips-and-techniques/bokeh-for-beginners.html.

32   Yorke, John. *Into the Woods: A Five-Act Journey Into Story.* 2013. The Overlook Press. Kindle Edition, 2015. p. 77.

33   "Berger, John." *BrainyQuotes.* https://www.brainyquote.com/quotes/john_berger_386439.

34   Kundera, Milan. *The Book of Laugher and Forgetting.* New York: Harper Perennial, 1978. p. 87.

35     King, Maggie. "Bokeh Photography: The Ultimate Tutorial." *PHLEARN*. 7 May 2019. https://phlearn.com/magazine/bokeh-photography-the-ultimate-tutorial/.

36     "Kokopelli." *Wikipedia*. https://en.wikipedia.org/wiki/Kokopelli.

37     Mills, Margaret A. "The Gender of the Trick: Female Tricksters and Male Narrators." *Asian Folklore Studies*, vol. 60, no. 2, 2001, pp. 237–258. JSTOR, www.jstor.org/stable/1179056. Abstract.

38     Cox, Jay. "Dangerous Definitions: Female Tricksters in Contemporary Native American Literature." *Wicazo Sa Review*, vol. 5, no. 2, 1989, pp. 17–21. JSTOR, www.jstor.org/stable/1409399. p. 20.

39     Sachs, Curt. "The Symbolism of Dancing." *Journal of the English Folk Dance and Song Society,* vol. 2, 1935, pp. 30–33. JSTOR, www.jstor.org/stable/4521060. p. 30.

40     Yeats, William Butler. *The Land of Heart's Desire*. 1894. https://en.wikisource.org/wiki/Page:The_Land_of_Heart%27s_Desire,_Yeats,_1894.djvu/28.

41     Carnazzi, Stefano. "Kintsugi: the art of precious scar." Translated by Francesca Clement. *Lifegate*. https://www.lifegate.com/people/lifestyle/kintsugi.

42     Labong, Leilani Marie. "San Francisco's master of modern kintsugi." *San Francisco Chronicle*. Web. 2 August 2019. https://www.sfchronicle.com/style/article/San-Francisco-s-master-of-modern-kintsugi-14276421.php.

43     Frost, Robert. "Nothing Gold Can Stay." *Poetry Foundation*. https://www.poetryfoundation.org/poems/148652/nothing-gold-can-stay-5c095cc5ab679. Line 2.

44     "Reach." *what to expect*. From the *What to Expect* editorial team and Heidi Murkoff, author of *What to Expect the First Year*. 22 February 2019. https://www.whattoexpect.com/first-year/reaching/.

45     Wilstach, Frank J., comp. "Innocent." *A Dictionary of Similes*. Boston: Little, Brown, & Co., 1916. Bartleby.com, 2010. https://www.bartleby.com/161/2450.html.

46     Plath, Sylvia. "Morning Song." *Poetry Foundation*. https://www.poetryfoundation.org/poems/49008/morning-song-56d22ab4a0cee. lines 16-8.

47     Frost, Robert. "Nothing Gold Can Stay." *Poetry Foundation*. https://www.poetryfoundation.org/poems/148652/nothing-gold-can-stay-5c095cc5ab679. line 8.

48     Styron, William. *Darkness Visible*. Kindle Edition. New York: Open Road, 1990. p. 66-7.

49     Clark, Austin H. "Nocturnal Animals." *Journal of the Washington Academy of Sciences*, vol. 4, no. 6, 1914, pp. 139–142. JSTOR, www.jstor.org/stable/24525845. p. 139.

50     "10 Really Bizarre Cocktail Names." *Liquor.com*. 6 May 2014. https://www.liquor.com/slideshows/bizarre-cocktail-names/7/#gs.tmz2o1.

51     History.com Staff. "7 Unusual Myths and Theories About the Moon." *History.com*. 27 August 2013. https://www.history.com/news/7-unusual-myths-and-theories-about-the-moon.

52     "photobomb, v." *OED Online*. Oxford University Press, June 2019. Web.

53     "photobomb" *Grammarist*. https://grammarist.com/new-words/photobomb/.

54     Yorke, John. *Into the Woods: A Five-Act Journey Into Story*. 2013. The Overlook Press. Kindle Edition, 2015. p. 73.

55     Campbell, Joseph. *The Hero with a Thousand Faces*. Princeton/Bolingen Paperback Third Printing Edition. New York: Princeton University Press. 1973, pp. 77-8.

56     Campbell, p. 82.

57     Boeckmann, Catherine. "FERNS, FOLKLORE, AND FIDDLEHEADS." *The Old Farmer's Almanac*. 9 April 2019. https://www.almanac.com/news/editors-musings/fern-folklore.

58     Bloom, Linda and Charlie Bloom. "The Real Reason That Opposites Attract." *Psychology Today*. 2 January 2014. https://www.psychologytoday.com/us/blog/stronger-the-broken-places/201401/the-real-reason-opposites-attract.

59     Yorke, John. *Into the Woods: A Five-Act Journey Into Story*. 2013. The Overlook Press. Kindle Edition, 2015 p. 115-6.

60     Borresen, Kelsey. "9 Signs You've Found Your Soulmate (If You Believe In That Sort Of Thing)." *Huffington Post*. 16 June 2014. https://www.huffpost.com/entry/finding-soulmate_n_5501502.

61     Keats, John. "Bright star, would I were stedfast as thou art." *Poetry Foundation*. https://www.poetryfoundation.org/poems/44468/bright-star-would-i-were-stedfast-as-thou-art.

62    Burns, Robert. "A Red, Red Rose." *Poetry Foundation*. https://www.poetryfoundation.org/poems/43812/a-red-red-rose.

63    "Metaphor." *Stanford Encyclopedia of Philosophy*. 6 September 2016. https://plato.stanford.edu/entries/metaphor/.

64    Springer, Shauna Ph.D. "How to Have your Partner's Back." *Psychology Today*. 2 December 2012. https://www.psychologytoday.com/us/blog/the-joint-adventures-well-educated-couples/201212/how-have-your-partners-back.

65    Jones, Andrew Zimmerman and Daniel Robbins. "String Theory." *dummies*. https://www.dummies.com/education/science/physics/string-theory-for-dummies-cheat-sheet/.

66    Spacey, Andrew. "Analysis of Poem 'Design' by Robert Frost." *Owlcation*. 28 January 2019. https://owlcation.com/humanities/Analysis-of-Poem-Design-by-Robert-Frost.

67    Okun. Alana. "How to Start Knitting (and Learn to Love It)." *New York Times*. 11 July 2018. https://www.nytimes.com/2018/07/11/smarter-living/how-to-start-knitting.html.

68    Hogenboom, Melissa. "We Did Not Invent Clothes Simply to Stay Warm." *Earth*. 19 September 2016. http://www.bbc.com/earth/story/20160919-the-real-origin-of-clothes.

69    "Un-Knitting or Tinking." *Wool and the Gang*. https://www.woolandthegang.com/how-to/knit/un-knitting-or-tinking.

70    "Tinkerbell Effect." *Wikipedia*. https://en.wikipedia.org/wiki/Tinkerbell_effect.

71    Shatto, Rachel. "5 Early Signs Of Emotional Chemistry, According To Experts." *elite daily*. 2 May 2018. https://www.elitedaily.com/p/5-early-signs-of-emotional-chemistry-according-to-experts-9038310.

72    Campbell, Kelly. "Relationship Chemistry: Can Science Explain Instant Connections?" *Psychology Today*. 21 August 2011. https://www.psychologytoday.com/us/blog/more-chemistry/201108/relationship-chemistry-can-science-explain-instant-connections.

73    Siegel, Ethan. "Ask Ethan: How Many Atoms Do You Share With King Tut?" *Forbes*. 14 May 2016. https://www.forbes.com/sites/startswithabang/2016/05/14/ask-ethan-how-many-atoms-do-you-share-with-king-tut/#79b2d97f71a5.

74    Weiss, Susanna. "Some People Relive Psychedelic Trips Years Later." *Vice*. 3 December 2018. https://www.vice.com/en_us/article/xwjv4a/some-people-relive-psychedelic-trips-years-later.

75    Baxter, Charles. "On Defamiliarization." *Burning Down the House: Essays on Fiction*. Kindle Edition. Minneapolis: Graywolf Press. 2008. p. 31.

76    "widow, v." *OED Online*. Oxford University Press, June 2019. Web.

77    Yorke, John. *Into the Woods: A Five-Act Journey Into Story*. 2013. The Overlook Press. Kindle Edition, 2015 p. 58-9.

78    Chadd, Rachel Warren. "The Folklore of Eggs." *Folklore Thursday*. https://folklorethursday.com/myths/folklore-eggs-mystical-powerful-symbolism/.

79    Dooley, Tristan. How to Read Nature. qtd in "Learn How to Read Nature with an Exercise From Tristan Gooley." *The Laboratory*. https://theexperimentpublishing.com/2017/10/learn-how-to-read-nature-with-an-exercise-from-tristan-gooley/.

80    Merchant, Nomaan. "Hundreds of children wait in Border Patrol facility in Texas." *AP News*. 17 June 2108. https://www.apnews.com/9794de32d39d4c6f89f-befaea3780769.

81    Romig, Rollo. "What Do We Mean By 'Evil'?" *The New Yorker*. 25 July 2012. https://www.newyorker.com/books/page-turner/what-do-we-mean-by-evil.

82    "Family Separation by the Numbers." *ACLU*. https://www.aclu.org/issues/immigrants-rights/immigrants-rights-and-detention/family-separation.

83    Romig, Rollo. "What Do We Mean By 'Evil'?" *The New Yorker*. 25 July 2012. https://www.newyorker.com/books/page-turner/what-do-we-mean-by-evil.

84    "Gravitron." *Wikipedia*. https://en.wikipedia.org/wiki/Gravitron.

85    Wilstach, Frank J., comp. "Force." *A Dictionary of Similes*. Boston: Little, Brown, & Co., 1916. Bartleby.com, 2010. https://www.bartleby.com/161/973.html.

86    "a force of nature." *Farlex Dictionary of Idioms*. 2015. Farlex, Inc. 15 Aug. 2019 https://idioms.thefreedictionary.com/a+force+of+nature.

87    "abstract." *Merriam-Webster Dictionary*. https://www.merriam-webster.com/dictionary/abstract.

88    "Concrete." *Dream Bible*. http://www.dreambible.com/search.php?q=Concrete.

89    *30,000 Years of Art: The Story of Human Creativity Across Time and Space*. London: Phaidon Press, 2007. p. 1038.

90    "Mnemosyne." *THEOI*. https://www.theoi.com/Titan/TitanisMnemosyne.html.

91    Berger, John. *Understanding a Photograph*. New York: Penguin, 2013. p. 100.

92    "Leeson and Russ 2018: Witch-trial activity across Europe." https://www.theatlas.com/charts/ByfNrXUBf.

93    Sartore, Joel. *Fundamentals of Photography*. The Great Courses. PDF. p. 179.

94    "Ono, Yoko." *Brainyquote*. https://www.brainyquote.com/quotes/yoko_ono.

95    Renner, Lisa. "Here's the buzz on missing bees." *Capitol Weekly*. 12 March 2019. https://capitolweekly.net/buzz-disappearing-bees/.

96    "Khloris." *Theoi*. https://www.theoi.com/Nymphe/NympheKhloris.html.

97    Purdy, Chase. "New data show the US honeybee population is still dying in record numbers." *Quartz*. 20 June 2019. https://qz.com/1649291/what-is-killing-the-bees/.

98    Ibid.

99    Woody, Todd. "Scientists discover what's killing the bees and it's worse than you thought." *Quartz*. 24 July 2013. https://qz.com/107970/scientists-discover-whats-killing-the-bees-and-its-worse-than-you-thought/.

100   "Flora 2: Plants of Greek Myth." *THEOI*. https://www.theoi.com/Flora2.html.

101   Gould, Wendy. "Dreams About Flying: Dream Meanings Explained." *Huffington Post*. 7 December 2017. https://www.huffpost.com/entry/dreams-about-flying_n_891625.

102   Taylor, Jeremy. *The Living Labyrinth: Exploring Universal Themes in Myths, Dreams, and the Symbolism of Waking Life*. New York: Paulist Press, 1998. Kindle 572-76.

103   Wordsworth, William. "I Wandered Lonely as a Cloud." *Poetry Foundation*. https://www.poetryfoundation.org/poems/45521/i-wandered-lonely-as-a-cloud.

104   "oriflamme, n." *OED Online*. Oxford University Press, June 2019. https://www.oed.com/view/Entry/132554?redirectedFrom=oriflamme#eid.

105   Mehta, Vinita. The Mysterious Power of Red." *Psychology Today*. 11 Dec 2014. https://www.psychologytoday.com/us/blog/head-games/201412/the-mysterious-power-red.

106   Ibid.

107   "What Is Black and White and Red All Over?" *Reference*. https://www.reference.com/hobbies-games/black-white-red-over-2e39d61c8431d4bf.

108   "The Sixth Sense." *Wikipedia*. https://en.wikipedia.org/wiki/The_Sixth_Sense.

109   "Red." *Wikipedia*. https://en.wikipedia.org/wiki/Red.

110   Honig, Bonnie. *Antigone, Interrupted*. Cambridge: Cambridge University Press. Kindle Edition. p. 9.

111   Ibid. p. 191.

112   Ibid. p. 193.

113   Burton, Neel. "Our Hierarchy of Needs." *Psychology Today*. 21 June 2019. https://www.psychologytoday.com/us/blog/hide-and-seek/201205/our-hierarchy-needs.

114   Ehlmann, Bryon K. "What Awaits at Death." *ResearchGate*. https://www.researchgate.net/publication/311794133_The_Theory_of_a_Natural_Afterlife_A_Newfound_Real_Possibility_for_What_Awaits_Us_at_Death.

115   Brautigan, Richard. *Trout Fishing in America*. 1967. Boston: Houghton, Mifflin. p. 5.

116   "Surreal Humour." *Wikipedia*. https://en.wikipedia.org/wiki/Surreal_humour.

117   from Monty Python's *Meaning of Life*.

118   Friedman, Thomas L. *The World Is Flat: A Brief History of the Twenty-first Century*. Kindle Edition. New York: Picador. p. 2.

119   "Modern flat Earth societies." *Wikipedia*. https://en.wikipedia.org/wiki/Modern_flat_Earth_societies.

120   Main, Doug. "What Would Happen if the Earth Were Actually Flat?" *State of the Planet*. Earth Institute. Columbia University. 24 January 2018. https://blogs.ei.columbia.edu/2018/01/24/flat-earth-what-would-happen/.

121   Smith. Belinda. "Lazy' pitcher plants catch more ants." *Cosmos*. 27 January 2015. https://cosmosmagazine.com/biology/lazy-pitcher-plants-catch-more-ants.

122    Ibid.

123    Ibid.

124    "Trap Dream Interpretation." *Dream-Meaning.Net.* https://dream-meaning.net/object/trap-dream-interpretation/.

125    "Quotes." *Goodreads.* https://www.goodreads.com/quotes/204193-i-live-in-my-own-little-world-but-its-ok.

126    "Quotes." *Goodreads.* https://www.goodreads.com/quotes/324426-for-the-two-of-us-home-isn-t-a-place-it.

127    Kloss, Kelsey and Danielle Fox. "25 Best New Year Quotes." *Decor.* 1 Dec 2017. https://www.elledecor.com/life-culture/entertaining/news/g3414/new-year-quotes/?slide=4.

128    Cartwright, Mark. "Prometheus." *Ancient History Encyclopedia.* 20 Apr 2013. https://www.ancient.eu/Prometheus/.

129    "insider, n." *OED Online.* Oxford University Press. September 2019. https://www.oed.com/view/Entry/96822?redirectedFrom=insider#eid.

130    "The Ten Best Kept Secrets of the World." *DiscloseTV.* 2016 June 30. https://www.disclose.tv/the-10-best-kept-secrets-of-the-world-311618.

131    "Top Ten Secrets of the World." *Top Ten Lists.* https://www.strangelist.com/top-10-secrets-of-the-world/.

132    Carsley, Sandy. "The 5 Best Kept Secrets That Most People Wonder About." *Kiwi Report.* 27 Feb 2017. http://www.kiwireport.com/5-best-kept-secrets/.

133    "13 World Secrets You'll Never Know the Truth About." *Brightside.* https://brightside.me/wonder-curiosities/11-worlds-secrets-youll-never-know-the-truth-about-386460/.

134    Jarus, Owen. "10 Biggest Historical Mysteries That Will Probably Never Be Solved." *LiveScience.* 6 Aug 2016. https://www.livescience.com/11361-history-overlooked-mysteries.html.

135    "The world's biggest mysteries scientists still can't solve." *News.com.au.* 3 Sep 2014. https://www.news.com.au/technology/science/archaeology/the-worlds-biggest-mysteries-scientists-still-cant-solve/news-story/aac87ed0bc09d5cd4dfba0d49f613334.

136    Bryant, Alison. "7 Ways to Develop Your Artistic Vision." *ALLWOMENSTALK.* 29 May 2014. https://inspiration.allwomenstalk.com/ways-to-develop-your-artistic-vision/.

137    Bourn, Jennifer. "Color Meaning: Meaning of The Color Purple." *BournCreative.* 5 Jan 2011. https://www.bourncreative.com/meaning-of-the-color-purple/.

138    Papineau, Lou and Andrea Swensson. "A guide to Prince's musical inspiration." *The Current.* 20 April 2017. https://www.thecurrent.org/feature/2017/04/20/a-guide-to-princes-musical-inspiration.

139    Deriso. Nick. "Prince Confronts the Jimi Hendrix Comparisons on 'Purple House': 365 Prince Songs in a Year." *Diffuser.* 8 May 2017. https://diffuser.fm/prince-purple-house/?utm_source=tsmclip&utm_medium=referra.

140    "Kenning." *Wikipedia.* https://en.wikipedia.org/wiki/Kenning.

141    Russell, Joyce. "Career Coach: The power of using a name." *The Washington Post.* 12 January 2014. https://www.washingtonpost.com/business/capitalbusiness/career-coach-the-power-of-using-a-name/2014/01/10/8ca03da0-787e-11e3-8963-b4b654bcc9b2_story.html?noredirect=on.

142    Szirotny, June Skye. "That Mysterious Influence of Naming." *George Henry Lewes Studies.* no. 62/63, 2012. *JSTOR.* www.jstor.org/stable/42827904. p. 90.

143    Whitehall, Jack. *Just One-Liners.* https://www.just-one-liners.com/ppl/jack-whitehall/.

144    Berry, William. "The Joke's on Who?" 17 Feb 2013. https://www.psychologytoday.com/us/blog/the-second-noble-truth/201302/the-jokes-who.

145    Austin, Michael. "Humility." *Psychology Today.* 27 June 2012. https://www.psychologytoday.com/us/blog/ethics-everyone/201206/humility.

146    Ma, Chris Jingchao. "Silent Rage: Queer Youth Self-Harm as a Protest." *The Journal of Speculative Philosophy.* vol. 33, no. 3, 2019, pp. 422–433. JSTOR, www.jstor.org/stable/10.5325/jspecphil.33.3.0422.

147    Urry, John. *The Tourist Gaze 3.0* (Published in association with Theory, Culture & Society) Kindle Edition. SAGE Publications. p. 2.

148    "Love, American Style." *Wikipedia.* https://en.wikipedia.org/wiki/Love,_American_Style.

149    "Catchphrase." *Wikipedia.* https://en.wikipedia.org/wiki/Catchphrase.

150     Friedman, Bonnie. "Relinquishing Oz: Every Girl's Anti-Adventure Story." *Michigan Quarterly*. 1996. 1-28. https://quod.lib.umich.edu/m/mqrarchive/act2080.0035.001/00000022.

## Acknowledgments

We are blessed to have so many wonderful natural, preserved places in our area. We are extremely grateful to the following:

Chanticleer Garden, Wayne, PA
Jenkins Arboretum, Devon, PA
Stoneleigh Natural Lands, Villanova, PA

Also, our travels brought us to several other gardens and wilds, including the Montreal Botanical Garden, a private residence in Wisconsin, and the area surrounding Telluride, Colorado.

For the incredible cover and interior design, we send huge love and appreciation for Michele Barnes. Also, for sharing her expertise, we are very, very indebted to Laura Ducceschi (http://thrulauraslens.com). Thanks also to Greg Miller, Nick Filone, Katie Montgomery, Mary Anne Harding, and all the fine folks at The Camera Store in Bryn Mawr, PA. And thank you, thank you Katey Schultz for the amazing editorial insights and suggestions; check her out at https://kateyschultz.com. Meg would like to give a very special to her mother and photographer Eunice Boscov for the inspiration, support, and artistic eye.

## Author's Bios

**Meg Boscov's** work has recently appeared or is forthcoming in galleries in Philadelphia, Media, Doylestown, Wayne, Wallingford, Haverford, and Ardmore, Pennsylvania. Before pursuing photography, Meg had many past lives: theatre, cabaret singing, dog training, and animal-assisted education. Meg founded Pup Up Social Learning, an innovative playroom/classroom where children team up with playful, certified therapy dogs. Children partner with certified therapy dogs to strengthen the child's social and emotional skills in a playful, non judgmental environment. Meg was also the co-founder of Mutt Match, a nationally recognized nonprofit service matched families with dogs in shelters and rescues. Mutt Match successfully matched over 150 dogs with loving homes. She is a graduate of Northwestern University.

**Randall Brown** is the author of the award-winning collection *Mad to Live*, his essay on (very) short fiction appears in *The Rose Metal Press Field Guide to Writing Flash Fiction*, and he appears in *Best Small Fictions* 2015 & 2017 & 2019; The Norton Anthology *New Micro: Exceptionally Short Fiction*; and The Norton Anthology *Hint Fiction*. He founded and directs FlashFiction.Net and has been published and anthologized widely, both online and in print. Recent books include the prose poetry collection *I Might Never Learn* (Finishing Line Press 2018), the novella *How Long is Forever* (Running Wild Press 2018), and the flash fiction collection *This Is How He Learned to Love* (Sonder Press 2019). He is also the founder and managing editor of Matter Press and its *Journal of Compressed Creative Arts*. He both taught in and directed the MFA in Creative Writing Program at Rosemont College and received his MFA in Fiction from Vermont College.